*The* Five Roles *of a*
Master Herder

## Also by Linda Kohanov

*The Power of the Herd: A Nonpredatory Approach*
*to Social Intelligence, Leadership, and Innovation*

*Riding between the Worlds:*
*Expanding Our Potential through the Way of the Horse*

*The Tao of Equus: A Woman's Journey of Healing*
*and Transformation through the Way of the Horse*

*Way of the Horse: Equine Archetypes for Self-Discovery*
*— A Book of Exploration and 40 Cards*

# The Five Roles *of a* Master Herder

## A REVOLUTIONARY MODEL FOR SOCIALLY INTELLIGENT LEADERSHIP

# LINDA KOHANOV

New World Library
Novato, California

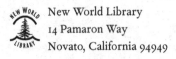

New World Library
14 Pamaron Way
Novato, California 94949

Text design by Tona Pearce Myers

Library of Congress Cataloging-in-Publication Data
Names: Kohanov, Linda, author.
Title: The five roles of a master herder : a revolutionary model for socially intelligent leadership / Linda Kohanov.
Description: Novato, California : New World Library, 2016.
Identifiers: LCCN 2016006216 (print) | LCCN 2016013516 (ebook) | ISBN 9781608683383 (hardback) | ISBN 9781608683390 (ebook)
Subjects: LCSH: Social intelligence. | Leadership. | Organizational behavior. | BISAC: BUSINESS & ECONOMICS / Leadership. | NATURE / Animals / Horses. | SELF-HELP / Personal Growth / General. | SOCIAL SCIENCE / Anthropology / Cultural.
Classification: LCC HM1106 .K6175 2016 (print) | LCC HM1106 (ebook) | DDC 303.3/4—dc23
LC record available at http://lccn.loc.gov/2016006216

First paperback printing, December 2017
ISBN 978-1-60868-546-2
Ebook ISBN 978-1-60868-547-9
Printed in Canada

 New World Library is proud to be a Gold Certified Environmentally Responsible Publisher. Publisher certification awarded by Green Press Initiative. www.greenpressinitiative.org

10   9   8   7   6   5   4   3   2

# Contents

# Preface

Learning to share power is the challenge of the twenty-first century. Men and women of diverse educational and economic backgrounds can access information and resources that were unavailable to them a mere decade ago. Today, anyone with a great idea can raise money online, order supplies delivered to the door, and conceive a multi-million-dollar corporation in the corner of a basement or garage.

In our global culture, it's not only journalists and politicians who disseminate information and share views. People around the world watch dramas as they unfold moment to moment, empathize, and join an international conversation that sometimes changes minds and lives.

As a result, command-and-control forms of leadership are suddenly less relevant — and on their way to becoming impotent and, finally, obsolete.

Still, after five thousand years of hierarchical, conquest-oriented models, it takes time, imagination, and experimentation to change old patterns. Blocks to success arise daily when people lack the sophisticated interpersonal skills to collaborate with coworkers, employees, clients — and family members, for that matter.

But we're on the right track. In the last twenty years, much has been written about the importance of emotional and social intelligence in the workplace — even in technical fields where geniuses proliferate. One ambitious study, undertaken by UC Berkeley, followed eighty-five PhD candidates in various *scientific* disciplines over a forty-year period. The results were surprising: High emotional intelligence (EQ) turned out to be *four times* more important in determining professional success than raw IQ and training.

As Bob Wall, author of *Coaching for Emotional Intelligence* and *Working Relationships* likes to say, "IQ and training get you in the arena; EQ helps you win the game." Just as physical conditioning takes consistency and dedication, emotional fitness doesn't happen overnight. But there's another challenge that raises the stakes considerably: We are, as a species, charged with rewriting the playbook for a whole new era of egalitarian sports, and the rules are changing fast.

## Glimpse

When I was promoted to a management position in the 1980s, there were no studies to legitimize what are still loosely, sometimes dismissively, referred to as "soft skills." The term "emotional intelligence" didn't emerge until 1990. It took another six years for Daniel Goleman to publish his influential book *Emotional Intelligence*. His equally important titles *Primal Leadership* (with Richard Boyatzis and Annie McKee) and *Social Intelligence: The New Science of Human Relationships* weren't released until 2002 and 2006, respectively. These and other books by authorities in the field have since sold millions of copies. Their popularity is a testament to something significant that went unnamed for far too long.

It's clear to me now, for instance, that a certain proficiency in emotional and social intelligence won me that first promotion to program director of a Florida public radio station. Three decades later, I asked my station manager, Pat Crawford, why he took a chance on me, a twenty-four-year-old classical music announcer. "You didn't just get along with your colleagues, you supported them in developing their own talents and taking creative risks," he told me. "You were out in the community, doing public presentations, making connections. You were constantly stretching yourself, encouraging others to stretch, and expanding awareness of the radio station in the process."

The backlash I initially endured over that promotion was significant. For the first two months, I ran a gauntlet of skeptical, sometimes-hostile reactions from staff members who tested me every chance they got. It was painful at times, but I became stronger. By standing my ground and refusing to hold grudges, I eventually won over the majority of my staff with an inclination to encourage and empower rather than rein in and ride herd over them. In this respect, our station manager and I were kindred spirits — to a certain extent.

Though Pat preferred to motivate rather than intimidate, he had no qualms about wielding overt authority, unapologetically, if other tactics proved ineffective with certain people. I, on the other hand, avoided anything resembling dominance, in large part because I had seen it so profoundly misused. This occasionally resulted in my supervisor having to step in when my more congenial style wasn't enough to handle conflicts between coworkers and to get uncooperative employees back on track.

I now recognize Pat's thoughtful, conservative use of the Dominant *role* as one of the marks of a mature, well-rounded leader. But it took me years to acknowledge the part this sometimes-dangerous "power tool" plays in the optimal functioning of any organization.

## The Elephant in the Room

Over the next twenty years, I worked in nonprofit, corporate, free-lance, entrepreneurial, and even therapeutic contexts, sometimes as a manager, sometimes as an employee taking an unofficial leadership role, and sometimes as a collaborator, educator, board member, or consultant. Over time, I began to see a pattern. Brilliant, well-meaning people who were technically accomplished in all kinds of fields had trouble getting along. While most said they felt stifled by traditional hierarchical structures, debilitating conflict all too often ensued when these same professionals were given free rein to question the status quo, experiment, and create something new with others.

While I expected this in highly competitive business and political settings, I was most astonished by the behavior of people in the caring fields. I encountered several experienced psychologists, for instance, who would wreak havoc in innovative situations where there was no officially designated leader. They could only seem to function well when they were either clearly the authority figure or deferring to someone they perceived to be in charge. While their patients loved them, these accomplished therapists simply could not collaborate with peers.

As a result of witnessing all kinds of unproductive behavior in corporate and social service fields, I continually searched for more efficient interpersonal communication tools, and I began teaching these skills to organizations and individual clients. Growing research on emotional intelligence certainly helped. Still, what mystified me the most was power, which was something very few people, myself included initially, were willing — or able — to discuss.

Most professionals avoided the issue, silently enduring the myriad dysfunctional ways that otherwise well-adjusted adults struggled to negotiate their needs and gain influence. Power plays abounded in the most benign situations — sometimes overtly, but more often than not through covert, passive-aggressive moves. It seemed that no one knew how to talk about the unruly bull elephant in the room, let alone teach him how to play nicely with others. Leaders and followers alike instead chose to ignore the musky, slightly pungent smell of that primal presence as they calmly drew their attention to the next point on the agenda of so many more important things to do.

## Horse Sense

Using power well is not a soft skill. Even so, it requires a sophisticated integration of leadership and social intelligence to channel potentially explosive forces into a focused and benevolent source of energy. I first experienced this delicate balance through working with horses, not people.

In the winter of 1993, I was living with my husband, musician Steve Roach, in Tucson, Arizona. Steve was away on an extended tour, and I had some extra time on my hands. After attending a few concerts and hiking down any number of cactus-lined paths, I decided to do something different: I took one of the many scenic-trail horse rides advertised around town. The experience was so serene, expansive, and invigorating that I bought my first horse, Nakia, the following weekend.

My intention was to ride into the desert to escape the sometimes-frustrating world of human affairs. Yet my beautiful, willful mare had something else in mind. Nakia, a striking Thoroughbred ex-racehorse, tested me every step of the way. Many of the tactics and strategies I had learned dealing with people didn't work with her.

Yet a strange thing began to happen. As I became more adept at motivating my horse, focusing her attention, and gaining her respect, relationships at home and work improved. People commented on the change, yet no one could pinpoint what had shifted. The plot thickened as I gained more knowledge about instinctual horse behavior. Based on my observations of how leadership, dominance, and cooperation work together in high-functioning herds, I began to notice nonverbal power dynamics between humans that were reinforcing unproductive patterns. What's more, techniques I used to gain the trust of unruly stallions worked equally well with difficult people. I suspected that with a little modification, I could even teach these skills to nonequestrians for use at home and work, but developing such a program would take some time.

Over the next eight years, I visited mainstream and therapeutic equestrian centers, interviewed experts in all kinds of related fields, studied a wide variety of riding and training techniques, and experimented with my own growing herd.

In 1997, through the many connections I made during this research, I founded Epona Equestrian Services, a mutually supportive referral service of riding instructors, trainers, body workers, educators, and mental health professionals who were interested in the healing potential of the horse-human bond. Some of the early members were counselors with a therapeutic orientation; others were innovative equestrians who wanted to help horses and riders lead more peaceful and fulfilling lives. I encouraged people to move beyond competitive forms of horseman-ship and explore the many benefits of working with these soulful ani-mals for the sheer joy, connection, and personal development benefits I was experiencing through my own close relationships with horses.

My first clients were equestrians dealing with "problem horses." In boarding, apprenticing, and later teaching at a variety of breeding farms and public stables in the 1990s, I could see that it wasn't enough for both species to become more physically and mentally balanced. They needed to be emotionally fit and socially aware. As I slowly be-came more successful at teaching nonaggressive leadership, mutually respectful relationship, and conflict-resolution skills, something pro-found — yet, from my point of view, predictable — happened to my human students. Their lives at home and work improved as well. And I began to revisit my dream of creating programs for nonequestrians to benefit from learning these same skills in safe, nonriding activities.

It was an exciting time. Still, the pieces needed to explain *what* people could learn from horses hadn't fully developed by the late 1990s. There was no widely accepted term for horse-related programs that proposed to teach personal and professional development skills in nontherapeutic settings — modalities that now proliferate under the umbrella of equine-facilitated learning (EFL). Back then, equine-facilitated psychotherapy was just emerging from the field of therapeu-tic riding, and mainstream equestrians were only beginning to accept the idea that horses were sentient beings with a dignity and wisdom all their own.

So you can imagine how hard it was to explain to people that while I was intrigued and most certainly inspired by the potential of equine-facilitated therapy, I was most interested in partnering with horses to help so-called "well-adjusted" people learn to how to *excel* in life and work.

## Stretching...Again

In 2001, my first book, *The Tao of Equus*, was published, and I was stunned by the response. Suddenly, I was meeting kindred spirits from around North America and across both oceans who wanted to study the techniques my colleagues and I had been developing since the mid-1990s. This sudden burst of international interest made it necessary to streamline these skills and teach them in two-, three-, or four-day workshops because our out-of-town clients wanted to have efficient, concentrated, life-changing experiences they could fit into a long weekend.

It was a tall order. Still, the formats and activities created in the wake of this new demand were an instant success: Participants not only came back for more, they urged us to start a facilitator-training program so that they could take this model back to their own communities. And so our regional collective Epona Equestrian Services became Eponaquest Worldwide.

A whole new set of challenges soon confronted me, however. The business grew fast. In 2005, I signed a contract to write my third book in the midst of leading four-day personal development programs, week-long facilitator trainings, and daylong corporate leadership workshops. At the same time, I was negotiating with an investor and moving to a large historic ranch that we were turning into an equestrian-based conference center. With a host of programs scheduled a year in advance, we had to construct that new facility in the midst of nonstop seminars as I worked on my new manuscript at night.

I invited a group of adventurous horse trainers, counselors, and educators to help with this multidisciplinary project, but it was like building a plane while trying to fly it. There were so many variables, so many areas where experts in different fields had to join forces to create something new. Once again, talented, technically accomplished people had to collaborate with peers in innovative settings, and it wasn't always pretty. This time, we had enough information on emotional and social intelligence to benefit in certain areas. Still, some essential piece remained hidden — and frustratingly, painfully, unspoken.

Over the next four years, I stretched in all sorts of contorted ways, feeling not so much inspired as kneaded, parboiled, and thoroughly baked by some mad chef trying to create new recipes from the same list of ingredients. My fourth book, *The Power of the Herd: A Nonpredatory Approach to Social Intelligence, Leadership, and Innovation*, grew out of the tools my colleagues and I developed as a result of stewing in that cauldron of advanced experiential learning.

In this effort, the horses were key. Because what we ultimately needed was an understanding of something long forgotten, something our ancestors had dropped beside the dusty road to civilization. Our four-legged colleagues were the only ones who knew the way back.

## Unexpected Wisdom

*The Power of the Herd* featured some of the principles that foreshadowed this discovery. In the six months between submitting the final manuscript and its hardcover publication, I developed what I eventually called "the Five Roles of a Master Herder," and I experimented with its effectiveness on clients and staff. This became the most popular feature of presentations and workshops I offered during my US and European tours supporting the book. In collaboration with my colleague Juli Lynch, PhD, I also created a self-assessment to help clients evaluate which roles they showed proficiency or talent in and which roles they were avoiding or abdicating. (See the Master Herder Professional Assessment, page 207.)

In doing research for *The Power of the Herd*, I found that for thousands of years, "Master Herders" in nomadic pastoral cultures had developed a multifaceted, socially intelligent form of leadership that combined five roles, which I call the Dominant, the Leader, the Nurturer/Companion, the Sentinel, and the Predator. This fluid vocabulary of interventions allowed Master Herders to move interspecies communities across vast landscapes, dealing with predators and changing climates and protecting and nurturing the herd while keeping these massive, gregarious, sometimes-aggressive animals together — *without the benefit of fences and with very little reliance on restraints.*

And I realized, at the dawn of the twenty-first century, this same nuanced approach to leadership and social organization must be resurrected if we hope to motivate modern tribes of empowered, mobile, innovative, and adaptable people to support one another through the inevitable droughts and doubts of life as we move ever more faithfully and confidently toward the greener pastures of humanity's own untapped potential.

## The Challenge

Employing these roles, consciously and fluidly, might seem like an overwhelming task at first glance, but I promise you, they're easy to recognize, even among citified humans. The average adult is already good at wielding more than one. But the idea of individuals developing and balancing all five of these roles for the good of one's family, business, and ever-widening local — and global — community promises something even more ambitious: a leap in the social evolution of humanity itself, helping large numbers of people to become empowered, fully actualized adults.

In this effort, we must *consciously* harness wisdom that nature has been promoting for millennia. In our sedentary culture, few people — even accomplished equestrians — realize that in herds of freely roaming herbivores, the Leader and the Dominant animals are often two different individuals, that they perform specific functions essential to the group's well-being, and that the other three roles also contribute to the healthy functioning of the social system — even when humans are not involved.

Still, most animals, *Homo sapiens* included, are drawn toward a couple of roles, while ignoring, avoiding, or outright rejecting the others. This tendency not only keeps everyone in a state of arrested development; it has a tendency to wreak havoc in challenging situations — unless the herd or tribe is managed by an exceptional leader who, like a

Master Herder in a traditional pastoral culture, is capable of employing the various roles as tools, rather than identifying with only one or two.

The simple, eternally irritating truth of the matter is that each role has a shadow side that results in dysfunctional behavior when it is over-emphasized. We're well aware, for instance, that people who cling to the role of Dominant or the role of Predator can become highly destructive in businesses, in families, and most certainly in politics. Your average dictator takes it one step further, combining the roles of Dominant and Predator and enslaving and victimizing people in order to thrive at their expense. But many people don't realize that these two roles are useful, necessary in fact, when separated and employed sparingly, for very specific purposes, by people who are well-versed in nonpredatory forms of power: people who know when and how to employ all five roles for the good of the tribe. For many people, it's also counterintuitive, yet ultimately enlightening, to realize that even the Nurturer/Companion role can have toxic effects in organizations and families when this function is overemphasized in an individual.

Still, it's important to emphasize that I gained proficiency in this model by working with herds of empowered horses *for over a decade* before I could codify and describe these skills, let alone use them consciously with humans. Saying that I invented the Five Roles of a Master Herder is therefore like saying Columbus discovered America. Numerous cultures were thriving in the New World long before this wily Spaniard washed up on shore thinking he had found a more convenient route to India. Similarly, the information I'm offering is actually very old, so old, in fact, that pastoral tribes throughout the world left this earthy wisdom behind whenever they, either by choice or force, traded nomadic freedom for sedentary security.

But one night, deep in the heart of the Arizona outback, I realized that my own horses had been silently tutoring me in these ancient ways for years, counting on me to reclaim this wisdom and use it fluidly — if only, at first, to save their lives.

# Introduction

The moon is almost full. Its soft light shines gold at the source, yet somehow turns blue as it flows over the desert landscape. The black horse paces back and forth, her labor pains increasing in intensity as her powerful mate mutters a deep, gentle sound of reassurance nearby.

Still, something is not quite right. Well before midnight, when most equine births occur, I sit down on a bed of straw and pat the ground, looking for some way to encourage the mare to rest for an hour or two. Surprisingly, miraculously, she lays down beside me.

Even so, Rasa's distress is palpable. She continually touches her nose to her hip, her gestures becoming so emphatic that I grab a flashlight and check under her tail. And there it is, one of many potentially deadly complications I was warned about: Though her water has not yet broken, Rasa's foal is emerging from the womb, destined to drown in amniotic fluid if I don't do something fast. I break the sac and support the emerging child, breathing onto his nose to encourage that first breath, relieved to realize the birth is not breech. By the time my ranch manager arrives on the scene, answering a concerned call I made to her not twenty minutes earlier, the foal is resting quietly under a canopy of trees, their leaves blowing gently in the warm September wind.

The tiny colt looks up at me, his eyes reflecting the rising moon. He stands quickly, easily, and ambles on shaky legs toward his two-legged midwife. The mare, however, is facing yet another challenge. She cannot get up. In fact, she doesn't want to try, in part because of a problem with her right back stifle (similar to the knee in humans) that was taxed to the limit by the stress of pregnancy.

Rasa's eyes begin to glaze over, and I feel tears welling in my own. Horses who can't stand can suffocate due to the increasing pressure of body weight on their weakening lungs. Somehow, my colleague Shelley Rosenberg and I have to inspire this mare to choose the promise of life with her newborn over the very understandable urge to sleep.

With Shelley guiding him from behind, the coal-black foal follows me like a shadow as I lead him toward his mother.

"Rasa, here is your boy," I say, directing the still-wet yet increasingly engaged little horse to breathe into the mare's nose. "You must get up now and feed him." The experienced mother nickers and suddenly comes to life at the soft, curious touch of her long-awaited second child. Yet Shelley and I exchange worried glances as Rasa struggles valiantly, then lies back with a weary, disturbingly defeated sigh. We know that we must *make* her stand before she gives up completely.

It takes two of us, one pulling a halter attached to a lead rope in front and the other pushing from behind, overriding our own fears and empathetic responses in order to increase the pressure on this exhausted mare. We progressively encourage, then insist, then demand that she rally every last resource she possesses to stay in this world. Finally through the herculean efforts of all three of us, Rasa leaps to her feet, shaking her mane in defiance at the specter of death slinking back into darkness.

Moments later, Rasa is caressing her boy, pushing him gently toward his first taste of milk. Indigo Moon drinks with delight as all the horses begin to whinny, welcoming another herd member into this strange and beautiful new world.

## Five Roles

To save the lives of both mare and foal, Shelley and I each performed four of the five roles of a Master Herder that night. Though it would have been tragic, we were also prepared to engage the fifth, if absolutely necessary.

In the days leading up to the birth, a number of staff members traded shifts in the Sentinel role as we kept watch over the pregnant mare, concerned that the long-standing lameness in her right back leg might lead to complications. Since horses usually give birth less than a half hour after breaking water, we knew we'd have to act quickly if there was a problem, long before a veterinarian could drive down the rustic dirt road to our ranch. While I was confident in Shelley, who had assisted in numerous equine births over the years, I also realized I needed to somehow overcome my notorious fear of medical procedures to learn not only what to *look* for but what I might have to *do* in any number of disturbing labor scenarios. It turned out to be a prescient move: While Shelley was planning to take over the watch at midnight, Rasa's foal emerged from the womb several hours earlier than expected — minus the classic signal that he was on his way.

Without the mare breaking water, it would have been deadly for the foal if I had stubbornly maintained the role of Sentinel, that is, if I had watched from over the fence and only called Shelley once something ran amiss, while abdicating a more hands-on approach because of my lack of veterinary experience. To read the subtle nonverbal communication Rasa exhibited during those crucial moments, I needed an intimate understanding of her unique behavior and a desire to comfort her. I needed to recognize that the *feeling* of concern my horse conveyed when she laid down was more than an early stage of labor. This intimate knowledge combined with my intuition came from years of close association and trust. Without my proficiency in the role of Nurturer/Companion, and the connection Rasa and I shared as a result, it's highly unlikely I would have been sitting on the ground next to her when the foal first emerged. The bond Indigo Moon and I developed as I helped him out of the womb also served us well in the years to come.

Yet this birth required much more than watching, nurturing, and supporting our four-legged companions. Shelley and I also had to engage two much more active roles that night, those of the Leader and the Dominant. We had to be quick about it, too. Taking the leadership position, I walked toward our first goal, drawing little Indigo forward, gaining his interest and cooperation without the benefit of restraints or training, compelling him to follow me around the corral to his mother as Shelley gently herded him from behind, taking the position of Dominant. When the feel and sweet smell of Indi's soft muzzle wasn't enough to inspire Rasa to face the pain of standing up, Shelley and I increased the intensity of these roles, simultaneously pulling and pushing, coaching, encouraging, and then demanding that the mare get on her feet.

Finally, if the situation had become dire, both Shelley and I would have had to accept — with deep courage and compassion — the role of Predator. We would have had to make the decision to euthanize Rasa. This would have been difficult enough, but if the vet could not arrive in time to humanely end our beloved companion's suffering, we would have had to use a gun normally kept on hand for protection in the desert outback and perform this most grievous and sacred act ourselves.

To this day, I thank our lucky stars we didn't have to engage all five roles that night. But our ability to incorporate and exchange the other four as needed offered me the first, most visceral glimpse of an ancient form of wisdom, one that has been all but lost in humanity's increasingly insulated, highly specialized, city-based, sedentary lifestyle.

## Power Struggles

Fall flowed into winter as Indigo Moon grew stronger and bolder with each passing day. His older brother, Spirit, was navigating the fretful challenges of adolescence, testing boundaries and finding ever-more-clever ways to amuse himself at others' expense. Luckily, I had some experience with disorganized male aggression. Both Indi and Spirit were sons of Midnight Merlin, a proud, at one time dangerous Arabian stallion who refused to submit to simplistic dominance-submission training methods.

Everything I feared and abhorred about the misuse of power was embodied in the patriarch of my growing herd. Merlin had been abused, in large part because *he* was defiant. Several trainers had tried to tame him with all kinds of techniques and tricks and intimidations — efforts that most often ended with some stunned, humiliated human scrambling to safety.

By the time I met Merlin, he'd been abandoned at a Tucson boarding stable and confined to an isolated corral. Though lonely and even depressed as a result, he was unable to control his own traumatized nervous system in the presence of horses or humans. A vicious cycle of terror and destruction swirled around him like a monsoon storm gathering force in foreboding yet unpredictable ways. Merely taking him for a walk was an ordeal few people were willing to face more than once. You could actually feel the thunder rumbling under the surface of his sometimes-calm demeanor. You just knew that lightning was bound to strike at any moment.

Thankfully, Merlin's tendency to rear up and attack without provocation lessened over the years of our association, and at times he was quite sweet. In the process of forging a partnership with him, however, I was forced to delve into the instinctual subtleties of dominance and leadership — and reflect on the ways in which both could be used to either build or destroy trust and cooperation.

This was initially a huge paradox for me. I was taught that power led to tyranny or, in women especially, ostracism. I spent years honing the tenuous combination of courage, compassion, mindfulness, and assertiveness that Merlin needed from me in order to find balance. It absolutely boggled my mind to realize that I was unable to tap the stallion's latent gentleness unless I could enter his corral with a strong yet caring presence, one that simultaneously didn't suffer fools, didn't hold grudges, and didn't take tantrums personally.

Yet just when I thought I had a handle on these issues, Merlin's sons came along and showed me that his tantrums were not, at their root, a reaction to abuse. These violent outbursts were more specifically an age-old call for skillful elders capable of helping younger generations socialize their own vast, untapped, all-too-often-misunderstood resources of personal and collective power.

Like their father, Spirit and Indigo were highly sensitive, naturally dominant, and extremely intelligent. For a time, they were even scarier than Merlin precisely because they had been raised in a secure environment. They had no fear of humans and were actually attracted to new things and experiences that would send the average horse running. Consequently, they would rear and kick and bite for fun, testing their strength and mine, but without the surge of anger I was able to sense in Merlin right before he would attack.

And so, it seemed, I reentered the school of hard knocks and scary stallions. Practicing various ways of channeling this tremendous energy and intelligence in productive ways — without lapsing into the negative, intimidation-based techniques that made Merlin such a troubled character — opened my eyes to a sophisticated, highly effective way of working with free, empowered humans.

Over time, I was able to translate the skills I had learned from my most challenging herd members into safe, efficient, yet exciting ground activities with gentler horses. I began teaching these tools to the executive teams, entrepreneurs, students, teachers, parents, clergy, and counselors who came to study leadership at my ranch in Arizona. In the process, I developed a nature-based model that helped people relate what they learned at the barn back to their offices, homes, churches, and schools.

As Spirit and Indigo Moon grew to adulthood, the once-aggressive colts became exceptional teachers of advanced students who wanted to tap the wisdom of these large nonpredatory power animals. All of us, the horses included, became more adventurous and collaborative as we learned to juggle the Master Herder's five roles. My clients were especially intrigued to discover that this innovative "new" approach was actually very old — as ancient as the human-animal bond itself.

## The Fittest to Lead

Charles Darwin's work suggests that it's not the strongest or the most intelligent of the species that survive, but the ones most responsive to change.

That means us, now, in this crucial, promising, yet precarious stage of our own species' development.

The sedentary, hierarchical, dominance-submission models of leadership the "civilized" world has relied on for the last few thousand years have outlived their usefulness. Ironically, the very technological advances this system once nurtured have given birth to an increasingly nomadic lifestyle where freedom, autonomy, and constant adaptation challenge all the previous rules of social engagement.

In the January 2015 article "20/20 Visions," *Entrepreneur* magazine asked leading futurists and cultural anthropologists to predict "how the next five years will revolutionize business." Brian Solis joined other members of the panel in emphasizing that "things are not only changing, but are so radically different that the business models we have today cannot support a much more dynamic approach to the market."

Shifting value systems demand innovation, not only in technology, but also in leadership as network-based organizational structures emerge. Younger generations are "very entrepreneurial and tend to have a lot of global connectivity," Bob Johansen observed. "They're very interested in environmental issues and sustainability." They also "want authenticity, they want transparency."

It makes sense. These are the people who will endure the effects of climate change and raise children in the face of dwindling resources. At the same time, their fluency in social media calls for collaborative business models that take advantage of "mutual benefit partnering on a global scale," or what Johansen calls (in his book by the same title) "the reciprocity advantage." For anyone born after 1990, hierarchical, highly competitive, slash-and-burn styles of corporate conquest are not only ineffective, they're simply less relevant. The most successful CEOs of the last forty years cannot model, and quite possibly cannot even imagine, the leadership and social intelligence skills the next generation will need to thrive in this brave new world.

## Power *and* Collaboration

While some corporate and political regimes still strive to disempower others for personal gain, relentless waves of technological, economic, and cultural innovation are eroding dictatorial resolve. In his book *The Third Industrial Revolution*, Jeremy Rifkin speaks of "an emerging collaborative age" in which "lateral power organized nodally across society" is "fundamentally restructuring human relationships, from top to bottom to side to side, with profound implications for the future of society."

There's one major issue we face in this transition: Far too many people experience power and collaboration as opposites, as if one must be sacrificed in favor of the other. Those who value power are more inclined to suppress collaboration to fulfill ambitious goals or reinforce the status quo. Those deeply committed to collaboration sometimes neglect assertiveness for fear of damaging relationships, even when a clear, directive, humane use of power may be necessary to motivate widespread positive change.

I once belonged to the latter category. Growing up female in the 1960s, before the women's rights movement gathered force and floated more gently toward my small, Midwestern city, I was encouraged to develop the nurturing arts at the expense of leadership. As I graduated college and entered the workforce, I was desperately untrained in the skillful use of power and influence, except through those genteel, primarily unconscious, passive-aggressive moves "the weaker sex" developed through five thousand years of subjugation.

In the 1980s, equal opportunity opened things up a bit. I could use intelligence, vision, enthusiasm, and degrees or certifications to be promoted, and I excelled at inspiring and collaborating with others — especially when working with self-motivated, caring people. But whenever it was necessary to make tough decisions, motivate uncooperative employees, deal with feuding factions, or lead others into controversial or uncomfortable areas, I tended to avoid conflict, at times abdicating authority when I needed to stand strong.

More dominant colleagues had no problem pulling rank, handling dissent, and herding others toward short-term goals, but these command-and-control-style managers were less effective over time. Many crossed the line between assertiveness and intimidation, losing trust along the way. Some withheld information and suppressed creativity, producing dull, listless staff members who hid growing resentment behind limp smiles of compliance.

If these leaders inspired anything at all in their employees, it was the tendency to choose between two mediocre options — to take their talents elsewhere or to become more complacent, in some cases machine-like, "retiring in place" decades before receiving that coveted gold watch.

## Pandemonium and Paralysis

When I began to teach emotional and social intelligence skills to a variety of entrepreneurs, corporations, and nonprofits in the early 2000s, I noticed that the gap between relationship-oriented and goal-oriented leadership styles widened in certain fields — which increased dysfunction. Social service, educational, and charitable agencies attracted plenty of considerate, openhearted employees, but these people didn't necessarily know how to get along. Unresolved conflict festered behind facades of politeness. Undercurrents of increasing frustration were expressed through skeptical silences in meetings and toxic whispers in the hallways.

Staff members who considered "power" a dirty word engaged in passive-aggressive moves to gain influence. For example, when differences of opinion and working style emerged, some people in the "caring fields" used the subtle, damaging ploy of undermining a rival's reputation by diagnosing him or her with any number of personality disorders, behind his or her back, usually while feigning concern for the person's mental health. This "armchair psychologist" power play successfully gained the person using it some followers — while creating factions that worked at odds with one another as a result. Yet those who employed this increasingly popular technique rarely acknowledged the unproductive results for the organization as a whole, let alone the personal ambition behind this divisive behavior. Instead, they saw themselves as victims or as self-righteous protectors of colleagues who were victims.

Highly sensitive people and abuse survivors, who felt called to these fields for the best of reasons, amplified stress in other ways. These employees were more likely to exhibit hair-trigger responses to minor threats or simple disagreements, take creative debate far too personally, and hold grudges. Such tendencies undermined working relationships, most insidiously because conflict-averse people acted out anger and frustration in secretive yet increasingly virulent ways, making it impossible for supervisors to catch difficulties in their earliest, most manageable stages. Simply by giving one another the silent treatment, for instance, key staff members could make it difficult for colleagues unrelated to the conflict to get *their* jobs done. Over time, more factions would be created, with each side feeling disrespected or undermined by the others.

Untrained in how to set boundaries, communicate their needs effectively, handle disagreements, and motivate others through unemotional yet compassionate assertiveness, leaders and followers alike had trouble fulfilling their noble goals, and the energy of idealism was depleted by the daily realities of interpersonal unrest. This made it difficult to serve clients, as well as to experiment, debate, and adapt to shifting social and economic climates — no matter how admirable the organization's mission might be.

Corporate and entrepreneurial settings, on the other hand, attracted more goal-oriented, technologically savvy people. These organizations faced a whole other set of challenges as people with great ideas and relentless ambition rose to influential positions without developing the emotional and social intelligence skills to lead effectively.

To make matters worse, brilliant minds were encouraged to ruthlessly compete with one another, most often through a combination of financial incentives and bell-curve firing practices, breeding mistrust, defensiveness, and the tendency to withhold important information from colleagues.

In the most extreme cases, a "kill or be killed" mentality focused on short-term profit at the cost of long-term company growth and sustainability. This led to all kinds of callous acts resulting from institutionalized predatory behavior. In one of the most famous examples — Enron — executives purposefully created a "survival of the fittest" culture, encouraging ravenous competition, not only with other companies, but within the corporation itself. Championed by Jeffrey Skilling, who served as president and chief executive officer, this philosophy promoted increasing aggression and, in some staff members, unethical business practices. As Bethany McLean and Peter Elkind observed in their book *The Smartest Guys in the Room*, traders and executives "who stayed and thrived were the ones who were most ruthless in cutting deals and looking out for themselves." The strategy backfired for everyone involved. Enron's subsequent downfall not only resulted in jail time for Skilling and other employees, but the company imploded at a significant cost to stockholders, employees, and society at large.

In politics, the gap between relationship-oriented and goal-oriented leadership styles evolved into a strange combination of pandemonium and paralysis as the twentieth century came to a close. To this day, social service concerns clash with competitive corporate ambitions on a daily, sometimes hourly basis, resulting in all the dysfunctions described above, acted out in a confusing free-for-all of unproductive behavior.

No wonder even the most well-meaning democratic governments can't seem to get anything significant done: The challenges that every modern organization faces are magnified exponentially when an entire country gets involved.

## Where Do We Go from Here?

In the last twenty years, a number of studies have explored "masculine" and "feminine" styles of leadership. From this perspective, command-and-control, task-oriented, winner-takes-all practices resulted from a long-standing preponderance of men in business and politics, a trend that ruled well into the twentieth century. Then, after women gained the right to vote and began to enter the workforce in increasing numbers, a revolutionary shift occurred. More collaborative, relationship-oriented, mutually supportive practices began to emerge as the daughters and granddaughters of the pioneering spirits of the women's movement gained advanced degrees, excelled in professional fields, and were promoted to management positions.

*Inc.* magazine's editor-at-large Leigh Buchanan divides the subsequent evolution of leadership into three rapidly shifting eras: the Age of Autocracy (ancient times into the 1980s), the Age of Empowerment (mid-1990s to the mid-2000s), and the Age of Nurture (mid-2000s to present). Buchanan describes this sequence in her June 2013 article "The De-Machoing of Great Leadership," but all three styles continue to exist side by side, allowing us to compare them in real time.

Modeling himself on samurai principles, Oracle's Larry Ellison is a modern poster child for the Age of Autocracy, "as he attacks competitors and pushes employees to the limit." Buchanan also cites General Electric's Jack Welch "for his propensity to get rid of employees while leaving buildings intact," gaining him the uniquely disturbing nickname "Neutron Jack."

To exemplify the Age of Empowerment, Buchanan cites Starbucks CEO Howard Schultz's strategy to "rely on store-level employees making decisions based on knowledge of their regions." She also looks at eBay's Meg Whitman "whose business model is all about autonomy, which requires her to trust people while insisting on integrity."

For the Age of Nurture, interestingly enough, Buchanan lauds the antics of three men: David Neeleman, who "dons an apron and serves snacks to JetBlue passengers"; Whole Foods' John Mackey, who "contributes $100,000 annually to a fund for workers with personal struggles"; and Tony Hsieh, who "enshrines honesty, humility, and weirdness among Zappo's core values."

"Increasingly," Buchanan asserts, "the chief executive role is taking its place among the caring professions. It takes a tender person to lead a tough company."

And, I would argue, it takes a tough person to lead a caring organization. But not in the way we usually define "tough." I'm not talking about a Larry Ellison or Neutron Jack. I'm thinking more along the lines of an Abraham Lincoln or a George Washington, two exceptional leaders who upheld controversial, socially conscious goals during exceedingly dangerous, pivotal moments in history.

What we're really talking about here is a long-standing, though initially slow-moving, trend toward *balancing* assertive, goal-oriented behavior and compassionate, relationship-oriented behavior that reached a tipping point in the late-twentieth century. In her June 2013 article "Between Venus and Mars: 7 Traits of True Leaders," Buchanan cites Lincoln as "a man for our times," one clearly capable of "merging masculine traits (strength of purpose, tenacity) with feminine ones (empathy, openness, the willingness to nurture others)." America's sixteenth president went to war to uphold his convictions, and yet his "humility and inclusiveness made possible the 'team of rivals' described by Doris Kearns Goodwin in the popular book of that title. Generous and empathic, he made time for people of all stations who approached him with their troubles."

Still, it's important to appreciate the level of *emotional heroism* it takes to combine "masculine" and "feminine" qualities, especially in challenging situations. In *The Power of the Herd*, I analyzed George Washington's impressive career in several chapters and came to the conclusion that in triumph — and, more importantly, in long, drawn-out periods of confusion and despair — he was a far more compassionate and inventive leader than most people realize.

"Let your *heart* feel for the affliction and distress of everyone," Washington advised. This was no small feat for a general who shivered with his troops and felt helpless as many of them starved to death at Valley Forge. Yet letters to trusted allies and friends reveal that he dealt with his own heightened sensitivity for years, struggling to maintain composure in the midst of searing empathic responses to the settlers he encountered during the French and Indian War: "I see their situation, *know* their danger, and participate in their *sufferings* without having it in my power to give them further relief than uncertain promises," he wrote to his British superiors in 1756, asking for support. "The supplicating tears of the women and moving petitions from the men melt me into such deadly sorrow that I solemnly declare, if I know my own mind, I could offer myself a willing sacrifice to the butchering enemy, provided it would contribute to the people's ease."

Though Washington was able to renew himself in Mount Vernon's pastoral embrace after the French and Indian War, rest and success did not make him complacent. As Washington repeatedly reentered public life, supporting one desperate cause after another, the turmoil he endured *voluntarily* is truly staggering. Rather than shield his heart against the disappointment, anguish, and sheer horror he witnessed, Washington remained steady and thoughtful in the midst of feelings that would have short-circuited the average person's nervous system. His was not the coolness of the sociopath who feels no fear, but the authentic hard-won calmness of a man whose emotional stamina was so great that he was willing to accompany people into the depths of despair, and *stay with them*, offering hope through sheer presence.

In situations that most leaders would find hopeless, Washington's unique combination of fierceness, fairness, authority, courage, self-control, and empathy kept people from lapsing into seemingly justified selfish, revenge-seeking, survivalist behavior. His open heart wasn't hardened by adversity, nor did it keep him from making tough decisions. He refused to coddle deserters or looters, ordering severe floggings of men caught stealing food. On rare occasions, he executed soldiers planning widespread revolt. And yet, he instituted a policy of humanity for prisoners of war, even as the British executed and tortured his own captured troops.

It's reasonable to say that Washington was one of those rare individuals capable of combining "masculine" and "feminine" forms of leadership, but it's more accurate to say he was a "Master Herder," someone capable of performing *five* crucial leadership roles fluidly, interchangeably, as needed.

In *The Power of the Herd*, I built a case for the fact that this at-once innovative *and* ancient approach to leadership stemmed from Washington's own experience taking care of large herds of powerful animals. He found and trained horses capable of enduring the challenges of war, and he rode and cared for all the others daily in times of peace.

Washington's ability to use the Five Roles of a Master Herder was developed over decades, though this nature-based wisdom supported his many goals at a subconscious level, like a musician who plays brilliantly without giving technique a second thought. He never wrote about using these skills — though the animals he relied upon would have demanded he hone this balance every day (just as my own herd introduced me to the same set of skills over two hundred years later). Even so, this experiential wisdom helped Washington become an exceptional leader capable of transcending the problems of a dualistic approach, allowing him to move beyond the human preoccupation with "opposites" like male versus female, power versus collaboration, mind versus heart, logic versus feeling, and assertive, goal-oriented behavior versus compassionate, relationship-oriented behavior. This ambitious, socially intelligent perspective is what our current, fast-changing culture increasingly asks both men *and* women to adopt.

The Five Roles of a Master Herder make sense of previously confusing group dynamics, while helping people to develop a mature, balanced, mutually empowering approach to leadership and social intelligence: at work, school, home, and in larger cultural contexts. This model helps us navigate change, handle conflict, and support innovation that serves the individual as well as the group, and perhaps most importantly, the health and well-being of all species and countless generations to come.

What more could we possibly ask for in this time of unprecedented, potentially dangerous, mind-bending possibility?

# PART I

# Artifacts and Origins

# CHAPTER ONE

# Evolution of Power

L ike many people, I've long appreciated the peace and renewal that
nature offers. But I'll never forget the day I first glimpsed the be-
nevolence, and highly adaptive intelligence, of the human-animal bond.

In the mid-1990s, I was boarding my horses at a rustic private facility located next to a large desert preserve. While I enjoyed exploring
the trails with my experienced cow horse Noche, I also looked forward
to quality time with Rasa, who couldn't be ridden because of a chronic
leg injury. Increasingly, the saddle collected dust as I took long walks
with my night-haired companion, letting her roam off lead to nibble
the dry, nut-flavored grasses as we meandered through a vast, primal
landscape. Occasionally, I would also invite my year-old, mixed-breed
dog Nala to accompany us, hoping she would soon develop the ability
to override her more aggressive instincts and protect, rather than chase,
the horses.

Rasa was well suited to assisting me in this task. While other herd
members would charge off at a gallop when Nala raced after them, the
black mare would trot a few steps and slow down to a walk, shaking
her mane in protest, kicking out slightly in warning, but never making
contact. Her restraint with Nala seemed intentional: Many times, I had
seen Rasa run coyotes out of her pasture, though her actions also had a

playful quality to them, as if herding small predators was a hobby she adopted for her own amusement.

One evening just as the sun was slipping below the horizon, the three of us were heading home after a relaxing, uneventful hike. Suddenly, Nala crouched down slightly, narrowed her eyes, and growled. Rasa raised her head and stared in the same direction. Moments later, announced by the sound of rustling leaves and snapping branches, a small yet imposing herd of cattle emerged from a nearby mesquite grove. I wasn't sure if the animals were merely curious or potentially dangerous, but I couldn't help focusing on their impressive horns as one of the larger females began to walk toward us with several others falling in formation behind.

At nearly eighty pounds, Nala was not a small dog. Even so, she turned tail, ran straight to me, and huddled against my legs for support, looking up as if to say, "What should we do now?" My only possible herding tool — Rasa's lead rope — dangled from my shoulder. Just as I was considering whether to stand my ground or carefully walk away, the black horse pinned her ears and lunged toward this rangy bovine contingent. The cows lowered their heads, backed up in synchrony, and turned away. Then, just for good measure, Rasa trotted back and forth in an arc, as if she were drawing a curving line in the sand, creating a protective bubble around Nala and me that was clearly not to be crossed.

I was astonished. Noche was the seasoned cow horse, not Rasa. If anything, I would have expected my dog to rush at the cattle as the mare ran home. For weeks afterward, my brain worked overtime, combining and recombining the "facts" I had learned about the "drama of survival." Ultimately, I was less confused by Nala's reticence to attack than by the question of why a herbivore, and a slightly lame one at that, would defend us both.

It took me twenty years to collect research capable of shedding some light on this event. (As in the case of emotional and social intelligence, pivotal studies on animal behavior that seem so obvious now simply weren't available in the 1990s.) Slowly, bits and pieces of the puzzle were revealed through multiple disciplines, infusing my writing with lots of questions and, thankfully over time, a growing list of answers that eventually allowed me to discern some useful patterns.

In part 1, I summarize and expand upon the most relevant theories and examples I presented in *The Power of the Herd* — ideas that in some cases challenge our most treasured, tenacious views about nature while foreshadowing a more balanced, mutually supportive approach to power. In the process, we'll revisit long-held misconceptions about the instinctual behaviors, emotional vitality, and intellectual capacity of all animals, including the talented, sometimes overly aggressive species known as *Homo sapiens*.

## Hidden Revolution

Most people are familiar with Charles Darwin's theory of natural selection. Related research by Peter Alekseevich Kropotkin, however, has virtually gone underground. The Russian geographer and naturalist published *Mutual Aid: A Factor of Evolution* in 1902. Over the next fifty years, the book was rejected, in some cases actively suppressed, by royalty, fascists, capitalists, and communists alike. Based on a collection of essays and magazine articles he wrote in the late 1800s, Kropotkin's observations of supportive social behavior in nature struck some corporate and political leaders as "dangerous." In fact, even before *Mutual Aid* made it into bookstores, Kropotkin was obliged to put his keen, insightful intellect to other uses, namely figuring out how to escape from jail.

The czarist-era Russian nobleman hadn't intended to cause so much trouble. Born a prince (though he rejected that title at age fourteen), he had significant connections and resources to draw upon. When Darwin's book *On the Origin of Species* appeared in 1859, Kropotkin was inspired to contribute to the scientific literature on this topic. Commandeering a group of ten Cossacks and fifty horses, he trotted off to Siberia, hoping to gather case studies to support and further define the intricacies of evolution. But soon enough, he was confused and disillusioned by what he saw — or perhaps more specifically, by what he didn't see.

"I failed to find — although I was eagerly looking for it — that bitter struggle for the means of existence, *among animals belonging to the same species*, which was considered by most Darwinists (though not always Darwin himself) as the dominant characteristic of the struggle for life, and the main factor of evolution," (italics added) Kropotkin wrote on the very first page of *Mutual Aid*.

He was even more disturbed by the fast-growing relationship between Darwinism and sociology, emphasizing that he "could agree with none of the works and pamphlets that had been written upon this important subject. They all endeavored to prove that Man, owing to his higher intelligence and knowledge, *may* mitigate the harshness of the struggle for life between men; but they all recognized at the same time that the struggle for the means of existence, of every animal against all its congeners, and of every man against all other men, was 'a law of Nature.'"

In Kropotkin's experience, this potentially destructive view "lacked confirmation from direct observation." By then, he had witnessed significant instances of mutual support and competition *avoidance* in the vast numbers of animals he encountered in the Siberian outback. Bears hibernating, squirrels storing nuts for the winter, and herds of large herbivores languidly migrating were the most obvious examples, but Kropotkin also noticed an even more profound theme emerging.

"The first thing which strikes us is the overwhelming numerical predominance of social species over those few carnivores which do not associate," he wrote, later adding that on the "great plateau of Central Asia we find herds of wild horses, wild donkeys, wild camels, and wild sheep. All these mammals live in societies and nations sometimes numbering hundreds of thousands of individuals, although now, after three centuries of gunpowder civilization, we find but the *debris* of the immense aggregations of the old. How trifling, in comparison with them, are the numbers of the carnivores! And how false, therefore, is the view of those who speak of the animal world as if nothing were to be seen in it but lions and hyenas plunging their bleeding teeth into the flesh of their victims! One might as well imagine that the whole of human life is nothing but a succession of war massacres."

Kropotkin insisted that mutual aid is not an exception to the rule; it *is* a law of nature. Supportive behavior, he wrote, "enables the feeblest of insects, the feeblest birds, and the feeblest mammals to resist, or to protect themselves from the most terrible birds and beasts of prey; it permits longevity; it enables the species to rear its progeny with the least waste of energy and to maintain its numbers albeit a very slow birthrate; it enables the gregarious animals to migrate in search of new abodes. Therefore, while fully admitting that force, swiftness, protective colors, cunningness, and endurance to hunger and cold, which are mentioned by Darwin and Wallace, are so many qualities making the individual, or the species, the fittest under certain circumstances, we maintain that under *any* circumstances sociability is the greatest advantage in the struggle for life."

Kropotkin's view of evolution subsequently moved him to social activism, though in this context his ideas were a bit too revolutionary. To find so many incidents of mutual aid and nonpredatory behavior in the animal kingdom was one thing. To become a vocal anarchist as a result of these observations was quite another. While some of his discoveries won him worldwide recognition as a geographer, he subsequently took on a decidedly subversive mission, disguising himself as a traveling peasant lecturer named Borodin to spread nature-inspired visions of social reform, encouraging peaceful collectives of free, empowered people living in decentralized systems. After landing in a Russian prison as a result of these antics, he continued to promote his ideas throughout Europe upon his escape. From Kropotkin's perspective, cooperation not only trumped competition in the drama of survival, it hinted at a deeper reality pulsing beneath the twentieth century's increasingly unbalanced obsession with instinct and intellect.

## The Beat Goes On

The heart, and all it stands for, is not a human invention. It's a force of nature.

Science prefers to dissect it and repair it. Religion alternately strives to promote it and control it. Art is unabashedly fueled by it. And yet leaders in all these disciplines have tried to hoard the heart's legendary wisdom by spreading, throughout history, the incessant propaganda that our species is the only one that feels, cares, suffers, yearns, loves — and therefore deserves to thrive at the expense of all the others.

At the same time, oddly enough, far too many leaders engage in activities that require suppressing empathy and connection. The Egyptians, after all, did not build the pyramids with compassion as their prime directive. From slavery and war to modern factory farming, child labor, and environmental devastation, conquest-oriented pursuits demand that people sacrifice their hearts to the glory of some brilliant idea, outlandish ambition, or intriguing profit-making venture.

In the late-nineteenth and early-twentieth centuries, the concept of evolution was used as yet another way to justify callous, opportunistic behavior. Co-opted by aggressive political and business factions that had previously used the divine right of kings and other religious metaphors to control the masses, Darwin's theory was reduced to slogans that promoted the *survival of the fittest* and *competition for limited resources* as laws of nature. Dictators, robber baron–style capitalists, and other human predators felt all the more inspired to develop "efficient" ways of exploiting resources, animals, and people who were touted as less evolved. Communism purported to level the playing field, but these experiments also failed as they relied on centralized control, suppression, and fear to gain "cooperation" in executing their initially idealistic plans.

The heart was missing in all these endeavors, reinforced by the notion that nature itself was an unfeeling, unintelligent, mechanical process. Darwin's writings, however, explicitly contrasted with this premise. "There is no fundamental difference between man and the higher mammals in their mental faculties," he wrote in his 1871 book *The Descent of Man*. As far as emotions were concerned, he also asserted that "the lower animals, like man, manifestly feel pleasure and pain, happiness and misery."

It took over 140 years for scientists to officially confirm this aspect of Darwin's theory. On July 7, 2012, "The Cambridge Declaration on Consciousness" stated "unequivocally" that "non-human animals have the neuroanatomical, neurochemical, and neurophysiological substrates of consciousness states along with the capacity to exhibit intentional behaviors. Consequently, the weight of evidence indicates that humans are not unique in possessing the neurological substrates that generate consciousness." The document acknowledged that "neural networks aroused during affective states in humans are also critically important for generating emotional behaviors in animals." This includes "all mammals and birds, and many other creatures, including octopuses."

Research in the late-twentieth century also confirmed Kropotkin's thesis that sociability is an important factor in survival and in the ongoing evolution of multiple species. There's even a biochemical basis for this inclination. The hormone oxytocin, which is present in all mammals, buffers the fight-or-flight response in favor of "tend-and-befriend" behavior. This powerful neuropeptide, once thought to be released only in females during labor and milk production, also appears in men when they engage in nurturing activities, including petting and caring for animals. In both sexes, oxytocin heightens learning capacity, social recognition circuits, and pain thresholds. It also helps heal wounds faster, lowers aggression, and creates a sense of connection and well-being.

The wonders of oxytocin have spurred further research into the long-term transformational effects of the human-animal bond itself, leading to an unmistakable conclusion: Caring for others is a part of nature that has taken on a life of its own, moving far beyond parenting direct offspring. Evolution has a heart. It's much more than a fleshy pump. We ignore its vast connecting wisdom at our peril. And we evolve in direct relation to how consciously we embrace it.

## Seeing Is Believing

Social media abounds with animal videos illustrating strong inter-species relationships and heroic acts of protection. Most striking, of course, are interactions between carnivores and creatures that would normally be considered food. In one popular scene, a polar bear gently plays with a Siberian husky. In another clip, a wild deer emerges from the woods to frolic with a large family dog.

"Well, that's easy to explain," one scientifically minded colleague told me. "Over thousands of years, our ancestors selected for friendly canines that could be trusted with our chickens, our sheep, our goats, and our children."

"But how do you account for the overtures made by the polar bear and the deer?" I asked in response. We both shook our heads in silent wonder.

In still another video, we see the stunning effects of oxytocin. An Irish barn cat, who has just given birth, becomes enamored with a group of ducklings nearby. With her system swimming in the ultimate bonding hormone, the feline's mothering instincts override her hunt-ing instincts. One by one, she carries the hatchlings back to her blan-ket, not to eat them, but to nurse them. And the fluffy yellow puffballs begin to snuggle, softly chirping, sipping milk alongside her purring newborns! As time goes on, the connection grows stronger, with the fast-growing ducks waddling behind their adoptive mother, towering over their feisty kitten siblings on morning walks to explore the farm.

Granted, these clips mostly feature domesticated animals that were bred to live with other species. But naturalists have also observed coy-otes and badgers hunting ground squirrels together, and zebras engag-ing in cooperative migratory activities with wildebeests. Beyond these scientifically validated examples, thousands of impressive amateur videos have captured supportive, even altruistic behavior among wild animals. Even though they may be willing to kill to protect their family members, however, large herbivores stop fighting when an aggressor backs off. This tendency to avoid fighting to the death, to "live and let live," is a major characteristic of what I've come to call "nonpredatory power."

## Juggling Clichés

Twenty years ago, I heard the first of many talented cowboys waxing poetic on what became a very popular theme. "Humans are predators, and horses are prey animals," he said during a well-attended lecture-demonstration. "And yet they allow us on their backs. Imagine that, letting a lion on your back! Isn't that incredible?"

Audiences rarely question this now-oft-repeated notion. However, this colorful yet simplistic interpretation of the horse-human relationship encourages experienced and amateur riders alike to ignore the daily reality of what both species are capable of. In the first place, humans are *not* carnivores. While some people habitually act predatory in just about any context, *Homo sapiens* are omnivores with a strange, sometimes-confusing mix of physical and behavioral characteristics. For instance, horses and other herbivores have eyes on the sides of their heads, emphasizing peripheral vision. Humans, like lions, look directly ahead, reinforcing a goal-oriented perspective scientists believe was designed for stalking. Even so, we have no fangs, and our nails can't rip through paper, let alone flesh. With the teeth and digestive system of a vegetarian, we have to cook our steaks and cut them into bite-size portions — if we choose to go that route. But we can also thrive on plant-based diets.

The problem is we've grown up in a culture of conquerors where predatory behavior is rewarded in far too many businesses and reinforced in far too many schools (especially in the highly competitive, sometimes-cutthroat world of higher education). Those who refuse to claw their way to the top often have trouble imagining an alternative because popular metaphors related to power are almost exclusively carnivorous.

The persistent image of humans as predators actually *disempowers* more sensitive members of the population. Remember, misrepresentations of Darwin's theories were promoted throughout the twentieth century to justify aggressive, opportunistic corporate and political interests. During that time, it was also useful to portray nonpredatory animals as gutless, anxiety-ridden prey. Gentle, caring people often follow suit, neglecting the skills needed to use power effectively, sometimes even accepting the role of victim because they can't stomach becoming a tyrant.

In nature, however, carnivores and herbivores both display intelligent, richly nuanced behaviors that contradict stereotypes. Horses, zebras, water buffalo, and elk will often graze relatively unconcerned as a predator who has recently eaten a big meal walks through their pasture. Yet when an agile carnivore is on the prowl, large herds will scatter long before the predator can get close. Nonpredatory animals conserve energy for true emergencies by assessing the intentions and emotional states of other species at a distance.

*This* is why horses allow humans on their backs. As we go through the various rituals necessary to ride them, they can tell we're not planning to eat them. But here's where it gets tricky for humans who deal in clichés. These agile, socially intelligent animals also understand the difference between mutually respectful, supportive behavior and aggressive, needlessly controlling behavior.

Dominant and/or more sensitive herd members have even higher standards for anyone who adopts the physically intimate leadership role that riding requires. It's also important to remember that horses like to play games with power, speed, boundaries, and assertiveness. Young stallions in particular are not at all shy about challenging a two-legged handler in the same ways they're accustomed to sparring with one another. Older, more experienced horses tend to be calmer and more accommodating around people, but they also know how to drive off predators.

In this context, it's especially important to remember that herbivores sometimes choose fight over flight, and not only when cornered. If you're naïve, presumptuous, or ornery enough to act like a predator in their presence, most will become evasive or even run, while others will attack. And heaven help you if you're dealing with a herd of empowered adult horses.

Kropotkin emphasized that the collective defense strategies of large nonpredatory animals are highly intimidating to even the most ambitious carnivores. "In the Russian Steppes, [wolves] never attack the horses otherwise than in packs; and yet they have to sustain bitter fights, during which the horses sometimes assume offensive warfare," he wrote in *Mutual Aid*. "If the wolves do not retreat promptly, they run the risk of being surrounded by the horses and killed by their hooves."

Large cats are more dangerous than wolves, of course, but lone hunters also know their limits. Recently, a horse owner named Talea Morgan-Metivier posted an astonishing nighttime video of a mare chasing a mountain lion out of a small corral — with her two-day-old foal trotting merrily beside her.

## Trance of Conditioning

These and countless other examples challenge our culture's most cherished beliefs about the drama of survival, opening up new possibilities, new nature-based metaphors, for a more evolved approach to power. Several uniquely human attributes currently hold us back, however. That big *Homo sapiens* brain we're so proud of can act like a steel trap, bolstering a species-wide tendency to cling to old beliefs that contrast with an ever-expanding view of reality. Scientists, politicians, religious leaders, and even horse trainers are guilty of this. For centuries, some members of these seemingly unrelated groups conspired to treat animals (and until very recently, women and minorities) as mindless, soulless machines.

Hoping to avoid the cardinal sin of anthropomorphizing other species, far too many researchers promoted a dismal, sometimes-damaging form of mechanomorphism — in extreme cases conducting sadistic experiments on "unfeeling" animals and "unevolved" races (and the Nazi experiments are not the only example, though they were among the cruelest and most disturbing). This is undoubtedly one of the reasons why it took well over a century after Darwin for the Cambridge Declaration on Consciousness to agree with him that all creatures possess some level of emotion and intelligence.

In 2001, during lectures for my first book, *The Tao of Equus*, the persistence of this mechanistic belief system was still apparent. People would occasionally walk out in disgust when I suggested that horses and other animals had feelings and were intelligent enough to move beyond pure instinct. Since then, hundreds of books and documentaries on the emotional lives of animals have swayed a wider public, but there's always a learning edge. Twelve years later, on tours for *The Power of the Herd*, I faced another round of resistance when I presented the idea that, as omnivores, we are capable of choosing freely between predatory and nonpredatory forms of power. Audiences on the whole were encouraged by this view, but some equestrians were dismissive, even hostile. I was surprised to find that a small but vocal number of people felt an almost religious fervor in categorizing all humans as predators, perhaps because the oft-touted opposite, "prey," was too horrifying to bear.

Built upon the deceptively efficient, sometimes-lethal combination of predatory power and mechanomorphism, modern civilization continues to indoctrinate humans into this steely interpretation of life in a thousand subtle ways. From the laboratory and the classroom to the boardroom and even the barn, stoic authority figures urge people to leave their feelings at the door. When ambitious leaders make decisions that marginalize others, the ubiquitous line "it's business, not personal" purports to absolve the aggressors.

What will it take to wake from the trance of our conquest-oriented heritage and reclaim the ability to choose among a much longer list of natural, mutually supportive, socially intelligent behaviors?

## The First Step

In this effort, it's helpful to appreciate the differences between carnivore, herbivore, and omnivore behavior, while recognizing "predator" and "prey" as *situational* designations. We sometimes forget that lions, wolves, tigers, and coyotes are also preyed upon — by other carnivores and by human trophy hunters. At the opposite end of the spectrum, fully empowered, adult herbivores do not act like victims in daily life. The young and old of *all* species are most at risk for finding themselves in the *role* of "prey animal." Their survival depends on the actions of courageous parents, siblings, pride or pack members, herd members, and even individuals from other species who put themselves at risk to protect the vulnerable.

Still, there are important distinctions between the assertive, nonlethal forms of power herbivores develop and the killing-consuming orientation of carnivores, though lions, wolves, and their domesticated cousins can also adopt nonpredatory behaviors, especially in relationship to animals and people they consider kin. Nature depends upon predators to keep life in balance with available resources, but through mutual aid, the hormone oxytocin, and the impressive protective abilities of potential prey, four-legged carnivores are prevented from decimating large herbivore populations. In trying to justify callous, sociopathic tendencies, conquest-oriented human cultures *overidentify* with inaccurate, cartoonlike images of humanity's status as "king of the jungle," using the idea that we are at the top of the food chain to exploit other species without reservation. The repercussions are reliably catastrophic.

To mitigate the dysfunctions that lead to war, economic crises, and environmental devastation, our species needs to cultivate an advanced knowledge of natural principles. In an act not unlike pulling ourselves up by our own bootstraps, we must learn to function more like ecosystems rather than rabid predators or meek and disempowered prey. If we cannot evolve, consciously, in this way, apocalyptic predictions will become a devastating reality, and life on this planet may reach the point of no return.

Here's the good news: A pattern for this transformation already exists, one that occurs over and over again, throughout history and around the world, whenever carnivores, herbivores, and omnivores combine forces through the process of *mutual* domestication.

## Made for Each Other

In 1992, Meg Daley Olmert, an Emmy Award–winning documentary filmmaker, was developing a series about the human-animal bond. Her interdisciplinary findings resulted in unexpected insights on how our ancestors formed associations with other animals, eventually resulting in interspecies partnerships that, in the process, changed the behavior and neurophysiology of our own species.

Olmert's years of dedicated research eventually led to her 2009 book *Made for Each Other: The Biology of the Human-Animal Bond*, which I highly recommend reading for its amazingly accessible discussion of interspecies evolution and, in particular, of the role of the hormone oxytocin in this process.

Over the last thirty years, studies involving rats, prairie voles, dogs, and humans have demonstrated that oxytocin makes mammals less fearful and more curious, encouraging individuals not only to form pair bonds, nest, and nurture their young but to leave the nest and explore unfamiliar territory, most especially new relationships. In her book *The Oxytocin Factor*, Swedish scientist Kerstin Uvnäs-Moberg, reports that "when given oxytocin, groups of rats of the same sex become more gregarious and less afraid of contact. As aggression in the group decreases noticeably, friendly socialization replaces it. Rather than avoid each other, the rats prefer to sit next to each other. This closeness leads in its turn to the release of still more oxytocin."

The hormone is increased on both sides of an interaction when mothers nurse their young, and when animals of any age groom one another. In undertaking her influential research to understand how the hormone works, Uvnäs-Moberg used oxytocin injections to isolate its effects. Subsequent experiments showed ever-more-startling results, including elevated pain thresholds, faster wound healing, and heightened learning capacity. But she could never fully separate oxytocin's influence on an individual's physiology from the hormone's prime directive: to calm and connect with others.

"Surprisingly, to a lesser degree, animals that live in the same cage but have not directly received the oxytocin also show the same changes," she marvels. "The other animals in the cage become calmer and have lower levels of stress hormones." Subsequent experiments showed that oxytocin's benefits could be spread not only through nursing and direct touch, but through smell, vocal tone, and the concentrated attention that mothers engage in when adoring their newborns and people exhibit in gazing at beloved pets. This potent little peptide has also been shown to dramatically increase focus and social memory, while making people more trusting and trustworthy.

As Meg Daley Olmert contends in *Made for Each Other*, "The triumph of trust over paranoia enabled humans and animals to come together in domesticated partnerships and emboldened people to move beyond the social limitations of kinship and tribe and live harmoniously in a civilized world.... When humans began to keep animals and animals submitted to our care, we inadvertently created a chemical biofeedback system that changed our hearts and minds."

Olmert's wide-ranging, multidisciplinary research also makes a strong case for the hormone's influence on people helped through animal-assisted therapy. Most significant is a 2003 South African study led by Johannes Odendaal and R. A. Meintjes showing that "when eighteen men and women interacted with their dogs (talking to them and gently stroking them) the owners' blood levels of oxytocin almost *doubled* — and their dogs were also twice as enriched with oxytocin!" Along with this rise in the hormone came a significant decrease in blood pressure and the stress hormone cortisol, as well as an increase in beta endorphins and dopamine.

Promising studies have confirmed that oxytocin relieves some of the antisocial tendencies of autistics and can help people with attention deficient hyperactivity disorder (ADHD) to calm down and focus. But the hormone doesn't easily pass through the blood-brain barrier, making pharmaceutical versions used in scientific studies problematic for daily use. "Repeated injections of oxytocin in high doses has been shown to affect the emotional centers in the brain," Olmert explains, "but that method of delivery is neither painless nor efficient. Nasal sprays also manage a degree of penetration. The problem is to reach the brain with the spray, you have to inhale almost three tablespoons of the substance. Even after all that unpleasantness, the effects are short-lived."

Nature's way is currently the only way for large numbers of people to benefit from oxytocin's impressive, multilayered effects. With this realization, however, comes an inescapable paradox: City-based life works at odds with the very biochemical processes that made our species less aggressive and more likely to collaborate with others. Citing psychiatrist and animal-assisted-therapy pioneer Aaron Katcher, Olmert observes, "In our abrupt shift from farm to factory, we did a lot more than just put down the plow. More critically...we broke the bond with animals that helped make us civilized human beings. Katcher sees the fallout from this sudden interspecies divorce every day in children who are too wild to participate in polite society," namely the increasing number of kids diagnosed with ADHD.

And what about all those hyperactive, hyperaggressive wolves on Wall Street? Wouldn't it be the ultimate irony to discover that after eons of evolutionary trends encouraging sociability and mutual aid, *concrete* jungles cause people to *devolve* into increasingly more vicious behavior?

## The Biology of Power *and* Connection

As decades of studies have shown, oxytocin buffers the fight-or-flight response, making mammals braver and more open to collaboration. But there's another hormone that adds just the right amount of spice to the mix, particularly in the context of leadership development. In

*The Oxytocin Factor*, Uvnäs-Moberg compares the "calm and connect" effect with a similar substance, vasopressin, which differs by only two amino acids. This behavior-altering peptide also encourages pair bonding, especially during sexual activity, but in a wider social context, it promotes a decidedly more active approach.

Vasopressin, Uvnäs-Moberg writes, "instills courage by making the individual feel aggressive and fearless. The rat, male or female, is prepared to attack, mark territory, and vigorously defend itself. Oxytocin instead fosters courage by diminishing the feeling of danger and conveying the sense that there is less to be afraid of. Animal studies appear to show that oxytocin has a special ability to make animals 'nice.' Physiologically, therefore, a substance related to strength and readiness (vasopressin) is a close relative to one that produces friendliness and caring (oxytocin). They function in different ways, and we need them both. As the popular Swedish fictional character Pippi Longstocking says, 'The one who is powerfully strong must also be powerfully nice.'"

Nowhere is this paradoxical combination exercised more dramatically than in nomadic pastoral cultures where people must nurture *and* stand up to large, potentially dangerous animals. Here, herbivores, carnivores, and omnivores up the ante on mutual aid, dramatically modifying their own instincts to collaborate with creatures that would otherwise be seen as enemies, competitors, or dinner.

Humans and herding dogs, for instance, must relinquish a territorial orientation to migrate with their grazing companions while also tempering aggressive behavior to nurture, direct, guard, and protect the entire interspecies social system. Tribesmen and tribeswomen must be brave, appropriately assertive, and alert around animals ten times their size. Cattle and horses must be respectful of children smaller than their own newborns, and they must refrain from running from, or attacking and driving off, "family members" that, in any other context, would be seen as potential predators. From birth, all members learn to respond respectfully to the subtle, meaningful, constantly changing body language cues of multiple species, suggesting that a particularly powerful combination of biochemical factors and behavioral modifications acted upon those of our ancestors who chose to form partnerships with large herbivores.

Meat provides a surprisingly modest part of the pastoral diet. Modern tribes mix grains, roots, fruits, and vegetables (gathered, traded, or planted and reaped during seasonal migrations) with lots of dairy products, everything from butter and cheese to fermented mood-altering drinks like koumiss, which Mongolia's nomadic horse tribes make from mare's milk. Some cultures, such as Africa's cattle-oriented Maasai and Siberia's reindeer-based Even people, occasionally consume blood from living members of the herd, though milk remains the staple. (Moving with the animals keeps these people physically fit — electrocardiogram tests applied to four hundred young adult male Maasai found no evidence of heart disease, abnormalities, or malfunction. Despite significant dairy consumption, their cholesterol levels were about 50 percent of the average American's.)

In the majority of these traditional cultures, cattle, sheep, goats, camels, horses, and other animals aren't treated as slaves or commodities, but as valued members of an interspecies society. Herders exhibit tremendous pride and affection toward their animals, who in turn trust their two-legged companions to lead them to greener pastures, oversee their mating, assist with their births, and milk them — the ultimate oxytocin-producing activity.

Close interaction with agile, nonpredatory animals promotes mental, emotional, and relational balance — as well as a form of empowerment that deftly combines fierceness and sensitivity. It is, after all, much more dangerous to herd, ride, or milk a large herbivore, even a domesticated one, than it is to hunt it from a distance. Interspecies affinity, attention to nonverbal cues, mutual respect, and mutual trust are literally survival skills for herding cultures.

## The Power of Observation

While archaeological records indicate that pastoral cultures gained increasing sophistication between ten and six thousand years ago, cave paintings suggest that humans and animals engaged in a much longer process of mutual observation, and this in itself had a transformational effect. In *Made for Each Other*, Meg Daley Olmert contends that quietly watching other animals could have jump-started the oxytocin response that eventually set the stage for interspecies partnerships.

Olmert emphasizes that oxytocin can be produced not only by touch but also by the highly concentrated focus that mothers show when adoring their newborns. She also thinks oxytocin may be released during the "hunter's trance," a term the evolutionary biologist Edward O. Wilson coined to describe an expanded state of awareness he encountered when observing animals in nature, in which heart, breath, and mind are quieted, resulting in heightened concentration and attention to detail. Still, it's significant that Wilson was *not* hunting in these cases, but watching ants and other animals with pure curiosity and no expected outcome. Wilson's choice to name this pleasant, slightly altered state "the hunter's trance" suggests that he hadn't differentiated between the intensely aware predatory stare of our hunter-gatherer ancestors and the soft, appreciative, inviting gaze of those ancient naturalists who were capable of actually bonding with animals.

In any case, once activated, oxytocin would have encouraged humans and other mammals to buffer the fight-or-flight response and take *social risks*, eventually boosting the impulse toward what Kropotkin called "mutual aid." Quite possibly, this boosted something else: A relaxed, concentrated focus, combined with intense dedication to and/or adoration of the subject matter, is also characteristic of creativity, suggesting that the biology of the human-animal bond could very well have been a factor in inspiring the earliest, most impressively detailed Paleolithic paintings at the Chauvet and Lascaux caves in France, some of which are over thirty thousand years old.

As David S. Whitley marveled in his 2009 book *Cave Paintings and the Human Spirit: The Origin of Creativity and Belief*, "This first art consists of true aesthetic masterpieces — works of art that fully rival our greatest creative achievements, of any time and place." At Chauvet, only one vaguely human figure can be discerned: the lower portion of a woman's body. A nearby image depicts a human-bison hybrid. The vast majority of the paintings are highly realistic, artistically accomplished representations of animals. But it also appears that the artists were able to get closer to some species, both physically and, more importantly, emotionally. Horses are the fourth-most-frequently painted subjects, behind felines, mammoths, and rhinos. And yet, these early equines are among the most vividly portrayed animals in the cave, clearly showing individual characteristics in striking detail.

One of the most famous paintings, featuring four horses, captures facial expressions that an artist would only pick up from close, direct observation of individual living horses. The smallest, most youthful animal has bulges along the bottom of its jaw — a classic sign of a colt or filly whose adult teeth are coming in.

Many of the lions also show specific facial features capturing intricate moods and behaviors, leading Olmert to come to a startling conclusion in her book: The cave artists "*knew* these animals — not just as a species but as individuals. These were neighbors, close neighbors." What's more, she insists, the "impressive detail and graphic skill" of the paintings "tells us those animals were not terribly frightened of us."

## A New Story

Most people assume that our ancestors advanced from hunting and gathering to traveling with domesticated herds. As the story goes, *Homo sapiens* finally settled down and claimed the land through agricultural innovations that, in turn, led to the invention of cities. Archeological evidence, however, reveals a much more interesting progression. Nomadic pastoralism was a specialization that grew out of early farming communities. For thousands of years, up until this very day in fact, migratory animal-centered cultures evolved beside sedentary forms of civilization, with each developing a unique body of knowledge.

Before we move forward, let me be clear: I'm not promoting one lifestyle over the other. I'm instead outlining a theory on the evolution of power itself, one that has an optimistic outcome. If we adopt the social intelligence and leadership skills pioneered by our nomadic cousins, while still valuing the technological innovations that could only have been perfected in a sedentary context, we may very well experience a transformation of consciousness that nature seems to have been promoting all along. Our very survival may depend on it.

First we have to expand our minds and tell a new story, one in which humanity becomes a partner, rather than a conqueror or director, in the coevolution of several intelligent species. This epic, far-reaching tale is not based on fantasy. Rather, it weaves together the latest findings on oxytocin, mutual aid, and the ability of herbivores to assess the emotions and intentions of carnivores at a distance, among other relevant insights.

## Origins

When people learned to till the soil, as any modern backyard farmer knows, they had to contend with all kinds of animals sneaking into those primal gardens. It wouldn't have taken long for fleet-footed herbivores like cattle and horses to begin orbiting around the edges of human settlements that planted grains. Yes, of course, these animals were hunted as well, but they were used to living with predators. They knew how to assess the moods of lone hunters as well as those that prowled in groups. Herd members in their prime were also confident that, working together, they could sometimes drive the aggressors off. When faced with the choice of eating low-nutrition forage in lion territory or nibbling on fields of wheat and oats in human territory, well, you do the math.

Without sturdy fences, early farmers needed to guard their crops during the growing season, though luring large animals close to home was an added benefit. Still, settlers found themselves shooing off more individuals than they killed for meat, and a new pastime emerged. Farmers and herbivores were both benefiting from agricultural innovations that satisfied their basic needs. In times of plenty, people and animals became interested in one another for reasons beyond sustenance.

Somewhere between the safety of the village and the unknown reaches of pure wilderness, adventurous members of the two-legged and four-legged clans met on fertile ground. More confident and gregarious animals approached humans who had a similar orientation. As these early naturalists looked at their wary neighbors with calmness, curiosity, and wonder — rather than fear, desperation, and predatory intent — horses and other large herbivores sensed that subtle yet crucial difference, and they relaxed and lowered their heads to graze. Feelings of fascination and accomplishment motivated these people to sit quietly at the edges of fields and invite the braver animals to take a few steps closer still. Eventually, someone held out a handful of grain.

Once the increasingly trusting animals were amenable to touch, oxytocin would have flowed between everyone involved in much higher doses. The effect of this contact high would have kicked in as individuals amenable to being stroked and groomed by another species returned to the herd and interacted with their shier companions. This more subtle release of the hormone would have encouraged the larger population to buffer the fight-or-flight response and begin to take social risks as well.

There were at least two other significant benefits for the human contingent: a rise in self-esteem and increased admiration from the tribe. In *Made for Each Other*, Meg Daley Olmert cites a study on this effect by zoologist Dale Lott, who surveyed visitors to a national park where hand-feeding wild mountain sheep is "a favorite pastime":

> Lott was interested in discovering why so many tourists were drawn to engage in this close interaction with wildlife. Overwhelmingly, those who fed the animals told Lott that they wanted to see the animals up close and find out if the animals could trust them. When questioned further, they reported that they actually felt better about themselves when a wild animal would eat from their hand. They also said they thought more highly of other people who were trusted by the animals and

that they felt their self-image was elevated in the eyes of others when a wild animal trusted them.

Here we begin to understand the simultaneous rush of connection and elation our ancestors would have felt under similar circumstances. But that was just the tip of the iceberg, as it turned out. Because those who were subsequently inspired to explore relationships with ancient horses and cattle would have found that they needed to move beyond the initial thrill of contact to become acutely aware, responsive, and powerful in ways that few people, even today, can fathom.

CHAPTER TWO

# Mutual Transformation

R iding a horse well is an art form; there's no doubt. But when I stepped out of the saddle to help my horses give birth, live as a herd, and socialize their children to thrive in the interspecies culture we were creating together, I experienced an astonishing variety of relational, psychological, emotional, and hormonal factors acting on me from moment to moment. For over two decades, I reveled, daily, in the oxytocin flow of trust and affection, both with mares and newborn foals and during quiet moments with my stallion and his sons. In standing up to unruly adolescents and dominant males, I felt the vasopressin boost of confidence and assertiveness. On several occasions, a more dramatic surge of courage and concern motivated me to put my life at risk to protect the horses (such as incidents with a bear and a couple of rowdy bulls). Other times, I stood, dumbfounded, watching Rasa chase cattle and aggressive horses away from me.

Eons ago, a rush of biochemical and behavioral agents inspired a leap in the evolution of multiple species. But it is no less potent when modern people step out of their insulated homes and accept nature's invitation to experience this transformation for themselves. To be equal with the herd — to strive to be as agile, alert, and socially adept as the animals themselves — is much more fulfilling than relying on restraints and extreme confinement to control a large herbivore's every move. As human beings learn sophisticated leadership and social intelligence skills from the animals themselves, the lines between species blur, and a paradoxical sense of power, humility, awe, and appreciation becomes the baseline for new adventures in connection and innovation.

But there's something else, something that borders on the mystical: A coordination of behavior and consciousness can sometimes make it hard to tell who is herding whom — who is teaching, who is learning, who is leading, who is following, whose idea it is to do this or that. Sometimes the human element is called to engage a more decisive, assertive role. But pastoralists from multiple traditions emphasize that you must be a faithful student and observer of the particular species, of the particular herd, and of the individuals that make up that herd to know when and how to take action. That means spending most of your time balancing the relaxed yet heightened awareness of a Sentinel with the intimate knowledge that comes from acting as a trusted Nurturer/Companion, rather than a stern and arrogant dictator.

I slowly became conscious of this nature-based wisdom while teaching leadership and social intelligence skills through equine-facilitated learning activities and, eventually, through workshops I offered that didn't involve horses. To better articulate these principles, I collected all the research I could get my hands on to understand what living with herds of large herbivores taught our ancestors. Archeological evidence was sketchy, but studies of modern Mongolian, African, Siberian, Middle Eastern, and European pastoral cultures revealed an incredible wealth of information, including how these interspecies societies deftly employ the roles of Leader, Dominant, Sentinel, Nurturer/Companion, and Predator to negotiate sometimes-fertile, sometimes-hostile landscapes.

In subsequent chapters, we'll look at the gifts and challenges of these roles and discover when and how to employ them most effectively. But first I'd like to describe how a balanced approach to using all the roles arose in pastoral cultures, where Master Herders juggled these skills daily to keep large, potentially dangerous animals together without fences, while also exhibiting minimal reliance on restraints. (For a fuller discussion of pastoral cultures, see *The Power of the Herd*.)

## Fulani Herders

In the 1979 article "Applied Ethology in a Nomadic Cattle Culture," Dale F. Lott and Benjamin L. Hart describe the insights they gained studying Africa's Fulani tribes as "a two-species social system," in which they viewed the Fulani tribes' unusually sophisticated herding techniques "against a backdrop of bovine social behavior."

The authors emphasize that sedentary cultures control their herds primarily by technological means: fences, barn stalls, halters, yokes, ropes, and bits that deprive "the animal of most of the alternatives that do not conform to human wishes." Factory farming is the ultimate example, as chickens, pigs, and veal calves are confined and harvested like vegetables in a greenhouse with no consideration for their needs as sentient, social beings.

An alternative approach to restraint "is to actively select the desired behavior from the animal's own repertoire and evoke that behavior." This means you have to be influenced by the herd before you have any hope of influencing its members, an astonishing proposition for anyone living in an anthropocentric culture. This is why, Lott and Hart write, in "European and North American farming, the use of this approach has largely been limited to intimidation or subordination, in which man controls the animals by assuming the role of social dominant."

Lott and Hart reveal that Fulani herders "may be thought of as taking a social role such as a dominant or a herd leader. Yet it may be more precise to describe them as exploiting the predispositions of cattle to yield to a dominant and to follow a leader." That might sound redundant, but remember: The "Dominant" and the "Leader" are literally *different animals*.

Just about anyone can recognize a dominant cow or bull in action. These animals assert authority by keeping other animals away from something desirable: food, water, females in heat, and so on. Dominants respond to the slightest hint of disrespect with immediate, sometimes-outlandish, corrections. On the upside, they also gain respect by breaking up fights between herd members, but sometimes, particularly in the case of adolescent Dominants, these animals will charge others for no apparent reason, keeping everyone a bit on edge. The group gives such individuals lots of space, looking away while preparing to *move* away whenever the saucy cow or big bad bull approaches. This, however, makes it hard for the Dominant to lead anyone anywhere.

Herd members capable of rallying the troops, on the other hand, exhibit the characteristics of what horse trainer Mark Rashid calls the "passive leader," though that term is somewhat misleading (as I've discussed in other books). The passive leader only appears passive to someone raised on the flamboyant, fear-producing intimidation tactics most aggressively displayed by adolescent alpha males, who are more often than not expelled from the herd until they learn to calm down and respect others. This is why in nature, young stallions, bulls, and male elephants roam in bachelor bands of heavily scarred individuals. Even among the most skillful pastoral cultures, male animals that cannot learn to temper their aggression are prohibited from reaching sexual maturity, becoming geldings, oxen, steers — or supper.

A male or female animal who deserves the distinction of Leader is a much more balanced individual who conserves energy for true emergencies. As I explained in *The Power of the Herd*:

> Certainly no pushover, he or she knows how to set boundaries without causing others unnecessary stress. Such an animal often reveals his or her potential early in life through a paradoxical combination of independence and sociability — only in this case, it's truly more of a passive sociability. Others gravitate to this calm yet still charismatic herd member, orbiting like moons around this individual's intriguing combination of curiosity, poise, and good-natured alertness (as opposed to hyper-vigilance). Yet while the leader enjoys company, he or she also exhibits a kind of take-it-or-leave-it attitude to the

herd dynamics others seem so invested in, content to wander off languidly to investigate something new, whereupon others trot over to check out what piqued his or her interest, causing the rest of the herd to follow in due course.

Though Lott and Hart didn't use the terminology of the Sentinel and Nurturer/Companion roles, the research team observed Fulani herders spending much of their day watching over the animals and "moving among the cattle at the camps, stroking their heads, necks, and the inner surfaces of the rear legs. The cattle interrupt other behavior to stand quietly for this grooming and even approach herdsmen and 'present' themselves for grooming or petting. Of particular interest is the rubbing of the inner surface of the rear legs. Adult cattle rarely groom each other there, but calves are regularly licked in that area by their mothers as they nurse. Apparently the herdsman is exploiting a property that persists into adult life but normally functions to strengthen mother-calf bonds."

## Mutual Socialization

Since the Fulani do not manage their herds on horseback, it's truly stunning to see photos of a tribesman or tribeswoman even *walking* comfortably among these massive cattle — who have unusually long, piercing horns — let alone grooming them, milking them, leading them, keeping them out of farmers' fields, discouraging fights between bulls, and thwarting aggressive behavior directed at humans.

In this context, it becomes clear that the Dominant role, when balanced with other, more nurturing activities, is essential in two major areas: assuring human safety and keeping the cattle from getting into all kinds of trouble. Breaking up fights between animals is one of the most dangerous yet productive ways of gaining the herd's respect as social Dominant, and this also guards against injuries that could easily get infected, since nomads have limited access to veterinarians.

To maintain safe relations with bulls known for bold and unpredictable behavior, Fulani herders must also use dominance to correct, immediately and dramatically, the slightest hint of aggressive posturing, especially when it's directed toward a human. Boys well under age ten are taught to recognize "broadside threats" and other more subtle signs that a bull is *thinking* of charging. When they see these signs, young herders are obligated to respond with an upraised herding stick and a yell, escalating quickly to a brisk charge and hearty smacks with the stick if the massive long-horned animal doesn't immediately back off. Considering the size, speed, and power of an irritated bull, submissive behavior must be obtained *before* the animal decides to attack or the human will have little hope of surviving such an encounter. Remember, the Fulani people manage their cattle on foot, not on horseback.

Even more impressive is the ability of Fulani herders to maintain fine control over large groups without halters, ropes, or other restraints. At the end of the dry season, when foliage of the uncultivated savannah is nearly exhausted, herdsmen allow grazing to the very edge of unfenced agricultural fields just as tasty shoots of maize and other crops begin to grow. Because herders have already established that they're capable of using dominance for benevolent purposes, these men rely primarily on vocal corrections and occasional charges at errant animals to keep them off highly desirable farmlands. In sharp contrast, Lott and Hart "observed several occasions when non-Fulani cattle handlers had great difficulty managing even one cow."

This advanced ability to direct an entire herd, however, depends less on training and more on *generations* of interspecies socialization. From day one, Fulani calves learn to respond respectfully to subtle changes in the body language of both species. As I've mentioned, tribesmen and tribeswomen must be brave, assertive, and alert around animals ten times their size, and cattle must be gentle and respectful of children smaller than their own newborns.

In Africa, the Fulani live among the most powerful predators on earth, so keeping calves safe is of primary concern. Some tribes go so far as to guard their young animals in camp as adult cattle move out to graze. While calves are nurtured and protected by both species at night, the tribe's four-legged children are led away from their mothers each morning after feeding and tied to a "calf rope." After the cows and bulls leave, these youngsters are then turned loose to move freely among the women, children, and older tribe members during the day, interacting with humans through a combination of loose informal encounters and purposeful episodes of restraint (when secured to the calf rope). In this way, social intelligence skills and mutually supportive emotional bonds are developed between the species.

At age six, Fulani boys begin learning how to wrangle their feisty bovine counterparts. As these novice herders struggle to move initially uncooperative calves away from their parents each morning, the boys also learn the wisdom of reining in and controlling their own wild impulses while gaining strength, courage, and confidence. Meanwhile, impressionable young cattle learn to respect two-legged creatures who seem to grow smaller with each passing day: During the first two years of life, calves practically double in size for every inch their human companions grow.

Finally, the animals themselves relax into a cyclical, predictable, yet varied lifestyle among their seminomadic human caretakers. While droughts can be harsh and stressful, adults of both species enjoy the varied terrain while orbiting camps that hold rest, security, and companionship at the end of the day. Knowing that everyone will reunite at sunset, calves do not show the kinds of exaggerated fear responses that fillies and colts in the United States exhibit as a result of being weaned suddenly and permanently separated from their mothers, causing the unnecessarily frantic behavior people consider normal in young horses.

Even among the Fulani themselves, however, Lott and Hart observe that

> it is not clear how herdsmen become able to act as leaders. Some felt that the cattle naturally follow a leader and would as readily accept the Fulani herdsman as a conspecific in that role. Other Fulani said that they had to train the herd to accept leadership. In such training, one herdsman called while walking slowly away while the other drove the herd from behind.

Eventually, this technique — which is a cooperative leading/ herding method undertaken by at least two people — results in reliable group behavior initiated by a single herder. Lott and Hart write, "Once [the herder] has the cattle's attention, he turns away and begins to walk, or even run, continuing to call as he goes. The cattle follow him in single file or two abreast, sometimes vocalizing." When the animals are all heading back to their children at dusk, the attraction of cooperating with the herder is clear, but the ability of a single herder to rally these animals with a unique call and lead them in a specific direction at other times of the day is impressive. In contrast, teams of cowboys in the American West use dominance to drive cattle from behind while on horseback, containing the herd on both sides.

As Lott and Hart conclude, "The adaptive value of following a leader seems likely that the follower benefits from the leader's knowledge of the terrain, food and water sources, and predators. At minimum, it favors group coherence while the animals are moving about."

## Art *and* Science

Depending upon the situation, Master Herders choose wisely between the Dominant and Leader roles, but they spend most of their time in the Nurturer/Companion and Sentinel roles. This is still true even of modern herders who otherwise lead a sedentary lifestyle. In *The Art & Science of Shepherding: Tapping the Wisdom of French Herders*, editors Michel Meuret and Fred Provenza draw together academic studies and contributions from expert herders in Europe, where shepherding is now a professional occupation rather than a tribal lifestyle. As the title suggests, the goal is to offer "scientific explorations of successful herding practices," but the authors also had to admit that there is an art to moving large groups of, in this case, sheep and goats through fenceless grazing lands.

Isabelle Baumont interviewed seasoned experts as well as novices just learning the trade for her essay "On Being a Hired Herder in the Alps." Competence in this field, she emphasizes, "is based largely on observation, which is the prerequisite for action." As a student herder named Celine told Baumont:

> You have to be constantly…on the alert, vigilant, so as not to overlook a ewe with mastitis or fail to notice that a lamb is missing.…I'm always amazed when farmers tell me stories of old herders who knew immediately if a sheep was missing, or that they thought they'd lost her at such-and-such a place. They're really observant; they never miss a trick.

Even so, *hypervigilance* is not a virtue. Nervous, indecisive handlers make the animals nervous. This encourages a needlessly panicking herd to flee or freeze during even the mildest of challenges and to engage in dangerous behavior during real emergencies. Poise, confidence, thoughtful assertiveness, and calm attentiveness are key qualities of Master Herders. If a shepherd overemphasizes the Sentinel role without proficiency in the other roles, he or she would be useless once the herd left the barn vicinity and moved into unfenced grazing lands.

Shepherds are Leaders when the herd follows them toward prime pasture and water. The human acts as Dominant when breaking up fights between animals, herding the group away from potential threats, or driving off predators. In both of these roles, however, shepherds must still keep in mind that they are primarily guardians and caretakers. For this reason, the Sentinel and Nurturer/Companion functions seem to be constantly running in the background through a calm, expansive awareness that senses subtle shifts in the herd and the environment. In this way, experienced shepherds adjust to the moods of the group, the needs of individuals, changes in the weather, and dangers on the horizon. Herders separate all of these roles from predatory power. The role of Predator is employed sparingly and reverently, such as to cull the herd (for sustenance and to keep life in balance with available resources) and to euthanize hopelessly sick or injured animals. As we'll explore later in this chapter, pastoralists eat much less meat than the average American or European. Wealth is measured, in large part, by how many healthy living animals the tribe or family owns.

Separating predatory behavior from the potentially aggressive Dominant role is especially important when traveling through open territory. A single-minded, heavy-handed, dictatorial approach can scatter the herd, requiring hours, even days, of extra labor to round everyone up again. To assess whether to employ the Leader or Dominant role — and how much motivational or protective energy to use — Baumont insists that herders "must be able to anticipate the flock's behavior well enough to decide whether he should take action, and, if so, what sort of action. Herding thus presupposes an in-depth knowledge of sheep so that the herder can adapt to ever-changing situations."

To achieve this ambitious balance, expert herders must combine power, courage, and alertness with responsiveness, humility, and concern. Moving the group is "a matter of perpetual adjustment between flock and herder," ultimately blurring the lines between who is leading and who is following. As Baumont contends, in many situations, "each party responds so sensitively to the other that there is no knowing which of them is dominant."

> The intimate association between human and sheep is integral to what herders say about their profession, focusing as it does on the hardships endured by sheep and herder, the places they have been together, and the rhythms of their shared existence. Listening to herders talk, an outsider begins to wonder whether they are not part of the flocks, so strongly do they identify with them.

## The Vocabulary of Balanced Leadership

Due to a lack of experience with free-ranging herds, civilized people blur the lines between dominance and leadership — and often associate power with predatory behavior. In forming partnerships with these animals, pastoralists learn to differentiate between the Dominant and Leader roles and to use each role for specific purposes. Herders also learn to separate predatory behavior from any form of power used to influence these animals. If former hunters had not realized how to do this, unfenced herbivores would have simply run away from overly aggressive humans.

When I teach assertiveness skills through equine-facilitate activities, highly sensitive clients initially refuse to engage the focused energy necessary to move a more dominant horse because, as they say, "it's too predatory."

Over and over again, I find myself emphasizing that in herding cultures, and among the animals themselves, the Predator role is *completely unnecessary* to the direction and protection of the group. For instance, when Rasa chased those free-range cattle away from my dog, Nala, and me, the feisty black mare was not trying to kill them and certainly not eat them. She was using the protective power of dominance to drive the massive interlopers off. The moment the cows backed away, she added a few emphatic gestures to underline that they should *stay* away, and then she calmly turned and followed me back down the trail.

Like most mature herbivores, Rasa eventually developed proficiency in several roles. She was a consummate Nurturer/Companion with her sons, and she used the Dominant role to fiercely defend them or direct them away from danger. In the wider herd, she became a thoughtful and confident Leader whom others chose to follow, especially in novel situations. Her other herd mates showed more inclination toward the Dominant or Sentinel roles, but they, too, developed solid nurturing and companionship skills, though most were less inclined to take on the Leader role.

Among herbivores, rare individuals will occasionally engage in predatory behavior. Some do so for constructive purposes — such as a mustang stallion mercy-killing a premature foal who cannot stand and nurse — and others for unnecessarily destructive reasons, such as certain zebra stallions who will sometimes kill healthy newborns sired by rival males.

As omnivores, humans have more pronounced carnivorous instincts that pastoral tribes learn to keep in check. In highly competitive, conquest-oriented cultures, however, the Predator role is overemphasized, even in nonlethal business, political, and educational settings.

For instance, when a manager uses others' vulnerabilities against them for personal gain, or when this person fires or lays off workers too quickly and callously, he or she is overemphasizing the Predator role. Learning to use this form of power consciously and sparingly, as Master Herders do, allows people to harness a potentially destructive force for life-enhancing purposes. In this effort, it's important to keep the entire "ecosystem" in mind. Carefully managing financial, environmental, and human resources involves a controlled and compassionate predatory wisdom that carefully considers what programs or business practices to cull for long-term sustainability. Using the Predator role unconsciously and without restraint, on the other hand, results in behavior that has less in common with a noble pride of lions than with the vicious, disorganized antics of a rabid junkyard dog.

## The Dangers of Unbalanced Leadership

As Master Herders learn the benefits of balancing all five roles, they also notice *unbalanced* behavior occurring in both animals and people who overemphasize certain roles. We commonly endure these same dysfunctions in civilized contexts where people are taught to specialize in narrow fields, and as a result, they mistakenly generalize this practice to developing *some* leadership and social intelligence skills at the *expense* of others.

Like aggressive stallions, command-and-control-style managers strut into rooms of employees that part like the Red Sea. These naturally dominant CEOs, politicians, teachers, and parents unconsciously assume that leading involves intimidating and/or micromanaging others. They tend to suppress collaboration and alienate staff, colleagues, and family members in the long run.

Other executives and community organizers overemphasize the role exemplified by herd Leaders (those animals that the rest of the group *chooses* to follow). Rather than actively driving the group forward or directing individual behavior, these visionaries inspire people to follow with good ideas and a strong yet welcoming presence that somehow stays above the fray. But over time, Leaders who refuse to pepper their style with the appropriate use of dominance *expect* staff to get up and follow them toward the next great idea on the horizon. When people are reticent to tag along for any number of reasons, unbalanced Leaders often report that "it's easier to do it myself." As a result, they become workaholics and/or tend to hire dominant middle managers to do the "dirty work" for them.

Adding to the dysfunction, Dominants and Leaders who lack the skills of a Nurturer/Companion have absolutely no patience for interpersonal difficulties that get in the way of their sometimes-lofty goals. If these same people also don't have a reasonable respect for the Sentinel role, they will miss important cues from the environment, market, and political atmosphere that alert them to unexpected dangers or opportunities that must be addressed for optimal success. Even worse, dictator-style executives and politicians who pair dominance with predatory behavior tend to "shoot the messenger," thus training employees or family members with important information to stay silent.

At the opposite end of the spectrum, those who overidentify with the Nurturer/Companion or Sentinel roles can be incredibly ineffective mangers, and they can be dismal parents as their children reach adolescence. In abdicating the Leader and Dominant roles, such people gain influence through passive-aggressive moves, including guilt-tripping, withholding important information, and attracting "followers" through gossip (undermining the subjects of these juicy anecdotes in the process).

When any of these roles are paired with predatory behavior, the group, community, family, or business as a whole suffers, especially long term. Even so, there is an important time and place for the Predator role: to keep life in balance with the available resources. People who overuse *or* abdicate this role can suffer incredible losses in business, especially when the economy changes. Those who overemphasize this role create the kind of mischief that led Enron's executives down a path of destruction. Those who refuse to engage the Predator, on the other hand, may neglect to cut expensive, low-producing programs and/or to downsize during lean times, endangering the entire company in the long run.

## How Pastoralists Negotiate the Predator Role

As I've said, pastoral tribes eat much less meat than the average American or European. Their wealth is evaluated by how many healthy, *living* herd members they have. Furthermore, because these people name each individual, nurture the vulnerable, and protect the herd with their lives if necessary, consuming the flesh of any animal is not taken lightly.

In these cultures, the Predator role coordinates, thoughtfully and compassionately, with the realities of the ecosystem. Mongolia's highly successful pastoralists, who raise horses, sheep, goats, camels, and cattle, cull animals in the fall that aren't likely to survive the harsh winter ahead, drying the meat to sustain their families until spring, while opening up severely limited grazing options to a smaller number of herd members. These people do *not* eat lamb or veal, even if a young animal dies of natural causes. Adults are also treated with reverence in death. Strict traditions insure that individuals are killed humanely and quietly, away from the herd, the women, and the children.

Culling the herd feels so much like a sacred trust that it becomes an important part of the tribe's religious beliefs. It's considered disrespectful, first of all, to waste any part of an older animal. Only the bones, which Mongolians believe house the souls of all living creatures, are left untouched, so that the spirits of cherished herd members can be released according to their own timing, to be reincarnated. (This means that dogs are prevented from chewing on bones.) The Buddhist-influenced tribes also believe that people sometimes reincarnate as "one of the five animals" — that is, horses, sheep, goats, camels, and cattle — and vice versa, lending an even deeper sense of sacrifice and communion to this symbiotic pact.

The close interspecies relationships herding cultures develop, regardless of differing beliefs about the afterlife, can also be glimpsed throughout the Bible. Yet the kosher code of the Jewish faith, in which a holy man actively blesses each creature before the slaughter, is the only remnant we have of this impulse in modern Western society. Orthodox tradition strictly forbids cruelty to animals, outlining the specific procedures, prayers, and spiritual mind-set for mediating such a sacrifice. Interestingly, kosher laws also forbid the ingestion of blood on the grounds that this would "comingle animal with human life streams." (When Jesus offered his blood as well as his flesh at the Last Supper, this powerful gesture would have been readily understood as the act of merging his life stream with those of his followers.) The Even people of Siberia, who believe they are half-human, half-reindeer, do in fact ingest the blood of their animals, as do the Mongolian pastoralists, who are perfectly comfortable with the idea of humans and animals reincarnating across species lines.

## A Dramatic Transformation

The intimate, mutually supportive association between two-legged and four-legged members of these tribes further explains why Jesus easily moved back and forth between metaphors in which he was depicted as a shepherd and a lamb. In fact, once you reconnect with Christianity's nomadic pastoral roots, the ritual of communion becomes a *multidimensional* symbolic act, designed not only to bring individuals closer to God but to keep the pastoralist perspective alive whenever and wherever city dwellers try to subjugate people and nature in support of a disconnected, materialistic cult of owner-masters. In this sense, Christ's paradigm-altering efforts to include non-Jewish people in the sacrament he created could also be seen as an attempt to balance the predation running amok in the Greco-Roman world, offering a potent transfusion of nonpredatory wisdom in the wake of increasing violence.

Extreme carnage wasn't just tolerated in Jesus's era; it was *cultivated*. The vast Roman Empire was managed by force and intimidation, and it was reinforced by sadistic "games" at the Colosseum: gladiator exhibitions, public executions, and "beast hunts," in which thousands of animals were slaughtered "with the right degree of cruelty." The

Roman historian Cicero praised this brutal style of entertainment for its ability to desensitize people to horrific acts, preparing them for battle. The fact that we now use our stadiums for football rather than blood sport is a testament to Christianity's effectiveness as an early form of social activism.

In the context of counteracting the Roman Empire's intensely destructive overemphasis on predatory behavior, Jesus's life is historically and culturally significant. He actively reinforced a nomadic nonpredatory philosophy at one of the most brutal times in history.

The sketchy details of his life underline his association with a herd-based philosophy. Jesus was born in a stable and laid in a manger. Shepherds and wise men — not opulent warrior-kings — were inspired to visit the newborn. Upon reaching adulthood, Jesus encouraged people to give up their possessions and wander the earth, letting God through nature take care of their needs, in large part through the profound interdependence of the human-animal bond. Ultimately, his method of influence came not through force, control, or even convincing intellectual arguments, but through communion — a ritual involving the human consumption of his flesh and blood.

At the last supper, Jesus metaphorically took on the role of a beloved herd member who gives up his life to sustain the tribe. During the crucifixion, he endured the harsh reality of this commitment. In an act of self-sacrifice filled with symbolic significance, Jesus transformed Rome's ultimate intimidation-torture tactic — death on the cross — into an image of triumph over oppression. This surprisingly effective gesture challenged the predatory basis of Greco-Roman civilization, and as a result, it shifted the violent trajectory of Western society as a whole.

If Jesus and his followers had only accomplished the eradication of Roman blood sport, that, in itself, would have been an admirable achievement. But over time, his story inspired increasing numbers of people throughout the world to temper other social systems that were based on cruelty, slavery, and carnivorous self-interest.

However, the movement was also negatively influenced by instinctual tendencies that are difficult to control in humans who overidentify with the Predator role. As Christianity was adopted by sedentary, hierarchical city dwellers, opportunists who had never experienced a herd-based lifestyle developed twisted versions of the religion to justify conquest and genocide. Understanding the pastoral roots and subsequent history of Christianity helps us make sense of the aggressive, predatory-dominant behavior we see some believers enact in direct contrast to the compassionate, nonviolent example Jesus set.

The assimilation of a nonpredatory, nomadic pastoralist religion into a predatory, conquest-oriented culture created a profound incongruence that causes some people to *lose* their faith as they watch others *misuse* their faith to oppress and intimidate others. To this day, however, many churches acknowledge their roots simply by calling their congregations "flocks" and their ordained ministers "pastors," a reference to the caring, responsive, powerful, and physically and emotionally heroic leadership that a shepherd embodies.

## Shadow Play

Unconscious overidentification with the Predator role is a serious secular issue as well. Forensic psychologists often describe the "predatory stare" of sociopaths. Animal abuse in particular is cited as *the* classic sign of a budding serial killer, though mental health professionals struggle with effective therapeutic options. Like psychopathic murderers, "sexual predators" are also considered untreatable in many circles.

To a much larger extent, unchecked predatory behavior wreaks havoc in business, politics, and even educational settings. When you hear people complaining that "it's a dog-eat-dog world," you know they're enmeshed in some sort of predatory power system. When therapeutic or personal-development clients say to me that they "don't feel safe in groups," I usually find out that they grew up in an intensely predatory family system or were bullied at school. As a result, they are hypersensitive to the slightest whiff of potentially predatory behavior in any social setting.

In "polite" society, the primary characteristic of noncriminal (though still unproductive) predatory behavior is *the willingness to use someone's vulnerabilities against him or her for personal gain*. In nature, predators are essentially hardwired to seek out the most vulnerable herd members because young, old, orphaned, or injured animals are the easiest to catch and kill. In a conquest-oriented society, this inclination is generalized to all kinds of nonlethal situations where people lie in wait to take advantage when someone lacks a skill set, is shy about speaking in public, makes a technical or interpersonal mistake, and so on.

By this definition, the press is intensely predatory, as are most politicians. But even mild-mannered people who overemphasize the Nurturer/Companion or Sentinel roles sometimes employ subtler versions of this predatory power play — partly because our conquest-oriented culture has conditioned them to do so, but primarily because these people lack understanding of how to use the Leader and Dominant roles in their constructive, *nonpredatory* forms.

A particularly talented "people person," for instance, knows how to support you and is sincerely interested in your dreams and struggles. Over time, you may grow to trust this person with increasingly more private matters. As long as you stay on this person's good side, the relationship feels incredibly nourishing. And it will remain nourishing — *if* the person is capable of using all five roles effectively to voice needs, set appropriate boundaries, and act assertively when necessary.

However, if this same employee, colleague, or family member has developed the Nurturer/Companion role at the expense of the other roles, he or she will employ passive-aggressive forms of influence. If you neglect or offend this person, he or she may pull back, give you the silent treatment, hold a grudge, or even seek a subtle, yet damaging, form of revenge: Since he or she *knows all your secrets*, this person is in the unique position to use a few choice vulnerabilities against you — usually quietly, stealthily, behind your back. In this case, the Nurturer/Companion is engaging a classic predatory power play — that of using others' vulnerabilities against them — as retaliation for a perceived wrong. An otherwise gentle, well-meaning person who employs this technique under stress will insist that he or she is the victim and refuse to acknowledge that the behavior is further exacerbating dysfunction. But this action breeds mistrust throughout the department, family, or wider social system by creating factions and demonizing the intended target, sometimes causing irreparable harm to a team or family member's reputation.

All of the roles have shadow sides that result in predictable forms of destructive behavior. People who overidentify with the Predator *habitually* use others for personal gain. Dominants can be inexplicably intimidating and abusive. Leaders can seem aloof and self-absorbed. Nurturer/Companions are masters at passive-aggressive manipulation. And if you offend or devalue a Sentinel, he or she is likely to withhold information and watch you struggle as a result, sometimes swooping in to benefit from your subsequent failure.

It's important to realize that in most situations, a person acting out in any of these ways is not defective or innately ruthless; he or she is *overemphasizing a role*. As this person learns when and how to employ the other roles, even someone who coworkers suspect might have a diagnosable personality disorder will show improvement. (People with serious mental health issues, on the other hand, need therapeutic support to show slower and in some cases more limited improvement.) Aggressive colleagues might simply be overidentifying with the Dominant role. Manipulative coworkers might be stuck in the Nurturer/Companion role, and so on. Understanding this phenomenon can help teams avoid the "armchair psychologist power plays" that people in conflict sometimes use against their colleagues, especially in social service fields.

## House of Cards

Still, there are people who consciously and purposefully take advantage of others. Sociopaths and psychopaths have little or no capacity for empathy or conscience. Luckily, most are highly impulsive, disorganized grifters who also overemphasize one or two roles, and they often slip up as a result.

A true evil genius, on the other hand, is another animal altogether. Like a Master Herder, he or she is likely to be proficient in all the roles and, most importantly, knows when and how to use each of them for greatest effect. Only in this case, even the Nurturer/Companion and Sentinel roles are employed with conscious predatory intent. And that intent is to *thrive* at the expense of others while destroying anyone who gets in his or her way.

A great example of such a (hopefully rare) individual is the fictional senator Frank Underwood in the Netflix series *House of Cards*, based on a novel by Michael Dobbs. It's fascinating to watch the main character, played by Kevin Spacey, employ the Dominant, Leader, Sentinel, and Nurturer/Companionship roles exclusively for predatory purposes — eventually reaching the presidency through the fluid and nefarious use of all five roles as needed. The series opener blatantly draws attention to his cool, sociopathic disposition when he dispassionately breaks the neck of a dog who has been hit by a car. Ending this animal's suffering turns out to be the only time Underwood uses the benevolent side of his otherwise calculating, at times depraved, predatory nature.

Master Herders, on the other hand, turn Spacey's portrayal of a slick, power-hungry psychopath inside out and upside down. These accomplished, socially intelligent leaders use predatory power for *non-predatory purposes*: for humane herd management and sustainability-related issues, including actual or metaphorical euthanasia (which will be discussed more later), and in general, for keeping life in balance with available resources. Master Herders take individual and group needs into consideration, employing each role as needed for the good of the tribe, the herd, and the ecosystem.

## The Ultimate Evolutionary Advantage

Gaining and maintaining a balance of the Master Herder roles, using them at the right time and right place, mitigates the dysfunctions that surface when a single role is overemphasized. If an entire group of adults or adolescents is encouraged to learn these skills, it becomes much harder for any individual member to manipulate, victimize, or take advantage of others. But that's just the beginning. As more people master these roles, increasingly higher levels of intelligence, adaptability, power, collaboration, and creativity are unleashed, and the entire social system elevates.

In part 2, we'll explore each of the five roles in depth and learn how to employ them to greatest advantage. However, it's important to keep several things in mind.

1.  Civilization's (sometimes-desirable) tendency toward specialization promotes gender stereotypes that people still enact unconsciously, even as many nations pass equal-opportunity legislation. Historically, men were taught to wield the Dominant and Predator roles at the expense of the Nurturer/Companion role. Women were encouraged to overemphasize nurturing behavior and actively discouraged from practicing how to use power effectively. As a result, "the weaker sex" learned how to gain influence through passive-aggressive manipulation, as did any male who was treated as a slave or serf. When some women join the workforce, however, they suppress the Nurturer/Companion role and adopt the unbalanced use of the Dominant and Predator roles pioneered by a "masculine," conquest-oriented approach to power. In both men and women, the Leader and Sentinel roles have been misunderstood and sometimes devalued.

    As a result of these factors, you're likely to be innately talented (yet quite possibly undeveloped) in certain roles, while being good at other roles because you were socially conditioned to be proficient in those areas. It's also important to notice which roles you ignore or actively avoid. Use the Master Herder Professional Assessment (page 207) to help discover your current gifts and challenges, with the ultimate goal of balancing all the roles.

2.  In exploring the shadow sides of the various roles, most people experience feelings of embarrassment, guilt, or shame in

recognizing the dubious, even hurtful techniques they've used to influence others in the past. If this happens to you, it is *absolutely essential* to realize that *you are not innately flawed*. Certain predictable dysfunctions arise whenever anyone overemphasizes a role. Once you learn to incorporate the strengths of all five roles, unproductive behavior will naturally fade, and thereafter it will only arise as an "alarm" that you are sliding back into old habits.

3. You may initially feel uncomfortable developing roles you have ignored or avoided. Again, our culture's tendency to specialize accounts for some of the resistance. Unlike technical or artistic fields, in which talent and focus in a specific area may be essential, leadership and social intelligence skills are more like reading, writing, speaking, using a computer, balancing your checkbook, and driving a car. You want to be reasonably effective at all of these skills to succeed in modern life. Even though some people may be particularly gifted in certain areas, becoming racecar drivers, bestselling authors, actors, computer programmers, or mathematical geniuses, the basic elements of these fields are useful to, and attainable by, the average adult.

4. Finally, it's helpful to clearly differentiate between predatory and nonpredatory power. For this reason, I've reprinted a chart from *The Power of the Herd* that illustrates this. Please remember, in nature, carnivores are not evil. They perform a valuable function. *Well-adjusted* lions, tigers, and bears also engage nonpredatory power during their interactions with family members. The Master Herder model takes this one colossal step further, asking us to *consciously* notice when we're falling into the unproductive habits of predators and, for the most part, to use nonpredatory power in influencing others.

| Predatory versus Nonpredatory Power ||
| PREDATORY POWER | NONPREDATORY POWER |
| --- | --- |
| Nourishes self at others' expense | Supports individual and group needs simultaneously |
| Values territory over relationship | Values relationship over territory |
| Values goal over process (The end justifies the means.) | Values process over goal (The end *never* justifies the means.) |
| Aggressive in taking others' territory and resources | Assertive in holding personal boundaries without ordering others around; migrates to avoid competition for limited resources |
| Attacks to protect self and others *and* gain advantage | Fights to protect self and others; prefers to herd family and companions away from trouble |
| Fight-to-the-death impulse is strong | Stops fighting when aggressor backs off |
| Conquest or survival-of-the-fittest orientation ("Kill or be killed" philosophy) | Mutual-aid or safety-in-numbers orientation ("Live and let live" philosophy) |
| Culls the weak (Must hide vulnerability at all costs) | Shields the weak (Vulnerable individuals can rely on others) |
| Leadership = dominance | Leader and Dominant are often different animals |

| Predatory versus Nonpredatory Power (*continued*) | |
| --- | --- |
| PREDATORY POWER | NONPREDATORY POWER |
| Rules through intimidation | Leads through experience, curiosity, and the ability to calm and focus others during crisis |
| Purposefully escalates fear | Conserves energy for true emergencies |
| Competition emphasized (Co-operates in group hunting and sometimes child rearing, though many species kill the young of other males. In some species males will kill their own young if not ferociously protected by females.) | Cooperation emphasized (Competition strongest among adolescent dominant-style personalities, though even these animals are tolerant of young herd members. Some bachelor horses will tend to orphaned foals.) |

# PART II

# Five Roles

# CHAPTER THREE

# Direct and Protect:
# Dominance without Malice

## *Role: Dominant*

Whether you overemphasize or avoid the Dominant role, learning to employ it *consciously* and *judiciously* is one of the most important — and difficult — skills to develop. A mature, well-balanced executive, community leader, or parent uses this assertive energy to direct others toward common goals, set boundaries, keep youngsters and adults out of trouble, motivate resistant individuals, break up fights, and protect the group from predators.

In working with large animals, Master Herders also cultivate a sophisticated knowledge of dominance to handle the flamboyant power plays that aggressive herd members engage to challenge authority and intimidate others into submission. Similarly, parents and teachers must help naturally dominant children modulate and channel this sometimes-explosive force into benevolent pursuits.

For anyone who deals with troubled teens, proficiency in the Dominant role is *essential*. Coaching all adolescents — from bullies to shier, more-sensitive students — in how to develop a mature approach to dominance is one of the greatest gifts that anyone who works with young people can give to future generations.

Here's the problem: Managing, let alone working for or living with, people who overidentify with the Dominant role is sometimes emotionally painful, intensely frustrating, and even occasionally dangerous. Teaching unbalanced alphas to use their power wisely requires considerable focus, courage, and finesse. In these efforts, you must not only be powerful yourself, but you must also model a centered, socially conscious use of this often-misdirected force — even if dominance is not your natural inclination. If dominance *is* your native tongue, you must transform your own instinctual tendencies to control, intimidate, and divide and conquer into an impeccable source of refined influence. Either way, it may be the challenge of a lifetime.

## Classic Dominance Games

To various degrees, naturally dominant people and animals experiment with using intimidation as a management tool. At best, they have strong opinions and aren't shy about directing others' behavior. The most dangerous Dominants, however, quickly escalate to violence while displaying an outrageous sense of entitlement.

Among domesticated herbivores, introducing new members to an already-established herd is dicey when adolescent Dominants are involved, particularly at mealtimes. If you feed ten horses ten separate flakes of alfalfa, those vying for supremacy will put on a hair-raising show, rearing and kicking, bucking and biting to claim that first pile of hay.

Within a day or two, the winner of this contest will saunter up unchallenged as the feed cart arrives. Yet if an immature Dominant secures the alpha position, he or she will habitually overcompensate to *maintain authority* — in part, it seems, out of amusement. That others respectfully yield as this horse moves to the head of the "cafeteria line" offers only a brief respite from the mischief he or she can perpetrate. After a few minutes, he or she will likely leave the feeding station to chase different herd members away from *their* hay, essentially using dinner as an opportunity to play "king of the herd."

An overly dominant horse will also attack others, sporadically throughout the day, *for no apparent reason*. This keeps the entire group a bit on edge so that everyone looks away and moves away when the proud mare, tempestuous stallion, or gutsy gelding struts through the center of the herd.

At the same time, a truly committed alpha *never* lets anyone move him or her around. In older horses, this particular game results in a predictable power play that can be safely used on humans as well. Unlike their adolescent counterparts, well-trained Dominants no longer try to intimidate two-legged caretakers, at least not overtly. Instead these deceptively calm, reserved animals plant their feet, refusing to budge when asked. Such horses are *not* lazy; they're challenging anyone who proposes to direct their behavior.

If you're capable of using assertive (rather than aggressive) forms of dominance thoughtfully and unemotionally, this regal herd member will cooperate. (More on how to accomplish this later.) Over time, such a horse will respectfully negotiate with you, sometimes deferring to your lead, sometimes drawing your attention to another option that's well worth entertaining. However, if you try to beg, coddle, punish, or rage at this animal, he or she will resist and most likely herd *you* around, in some cases so gently and decisively that you momentarily forget what you were planning to do to begin with. Some accomplished Dominants are downright seductive in the ways they get inexperienced caretakers to do their bidding.

## Two-Legged Dominants

Humans who overemphasize dominance play similar games, though most of these people are unconscious of what they're doing and how they affect others. To some high-powered CEOs, intensely autocratic behavior becomes their baseline — usually through a combination of talent for this role reinforced by parental encouragement, followed by success in competitive educational environments and cutthroat business climates. At times, the tendency to maintain power by attacking others for little or no reason is so innate that such people often don't even *remember* insulting a colleague or employee in a meeting or notice the stress this creates in everyone else sitting at the table.

Naturally dominant children and employees constantly challenge authority. These people sometimes rule the roost unofficially by intimidating the designated leader into submission. If they can't get away with overt power plays, they'll intentionally neglect to do what parents, teachers, bosses, and colleagues ask, modeling the behavior of dominant horses who use the same technique to quietly toy with their two-legged handlers.

Among human Dominants, the ability to launch glib and clever verbal jabs at coworkers or family members is a nonviolent way of attacking others for no apparent reason. Such people label anyone who objects to this treatment as "too sensitive" and will sometimes consider it part of their mission to "toughen this person up."

However, an immature Dominant's definition of "tough" is rudimentary and often counterproductive. In settings where people are free to come and go, many choose to *go* when autocratic alphas hold influential positions. Community groups, parent-teacher associations, churches, and entrepreneurial endeavors lose valuable members when well-meaning leaders and board members cannot modulate the behavior of aggressive, controlling volunteers and staff members.

In the corporate world, large salaries still entice many workers to endure intensely competitive, demeaning bosses. Younger generations, however, are less tolerant of disrespectful power plays and "my way or the highway" tactics. Talented, independent people are more than happy to "hit the road" in these situations, especially when the internet makes it easier to work from home and start a business online.

Still, some overly dominant executives are quite conscious of what they're doing, even as they ignore the long-term repercussions. One of my clients found herself sitting next to the CEO of a Fortune 500 company on her way to an advanced workshop. In preparation, she was reading *The Power of the Herd* on the plane when this charismatic, well-dressed man asked her why she was traveling to Tucson.

"I told him I was going to a special training to practice leadership skills by working with horses," she remembered. "He laughed and said that he could tell me everything I needed to know about leadership in ten minutes. The man proceeded to outline the characteristics of instinctually dominant behavior as if it were a management philosophy that he came up with! I mean he actually recommended that I pick someone in every meeting — it didn't matter who, he said — and give this person a bit of a hard time, call him or her on the carpet for something. This way, he assured me, people would sit up, pay attention, and never take advantage of me."

## Instinctual Characteristics of an Immature Human or Animal Dominant

In the part 2 chapters, I list a variety of characteristics, benefits, and challenges for those who emphasize each role. These lists distinguish between qualities that are common in both humans and animals and those that apply only to humans.

Uses intimidation as a management tool.

Exhibits a strong sense of entitlement.

Often asserts power divisively, usually by keeping others away from something valuable (food, water, resources, mares in heat, and so on).

Sometimes attacks others for little or no reason (to keep everyone a bit on edge).

Pressures others to yield, to look away or move away as a sign of respect.

Refuses to move when others ask.

Herds others with a driving force, most often by pushing the group from behind.

Exhibits tendencies to micromanage, demand compliance, and control others' behavior.

Verbally or nonverbally expresses a "my way or the highway" attitude.

## The Challenge of Dominance

When undeveloped, the instinctual impulses of Dominants can be harsh and oppressive. Because they push others around and occasionally launch undeserved attacks, they are the most-feared, least-trusted herd members.

That the group is conditioned to *move away* from the Dominant allows him or her to drive others away from danger or toward a goal. But no one *chooses* to follow individuals who overemphasize this role. Consequently, it's difficult for Dominants to lead anyone anywhere, especially in novel situations. In a crisis, immature Dominants increase panic and decrease thoughtful problem-solving abilities. As a result, they don't function well in innovative settings, and they often resist change because reinforcing the status quo offers them more control.

## Optimal Use of Dominance

However, when dominance is used consciously — in balance with skills developed through exercising the other roles — it becomes a constructive force for motivating others and moderating unproductive group behavior. Mature Dominants transform their potentially explosive energy into a "direct-and-protect" orientation, deftly employing the role's *divisive* and *driving* forces for specific, life-enhancing pursuits. While their adolescent counterparts are busy chasing herd members away from food and water, horses who master this role use their refined, still-potent power to break up fights between individuals (divisive), set boundaries with aggressors (divisive), herd the group away from danger (divisive and driving), and chase off predators (driving).

In pastoral cultures, expert herders employ dominance for these same purposes, while helping their younger counterparts convert disorganized aggression into focused, intelligent assertiveness. During seasonal migrations, Fulani herders regularly employ the *divisive* energy of this role to keep loose cattle out of farmers' unfenced fields, thus preventing war with the tribe's sedentary neighbors.

Accomplished human leaders use the Dominant's *driving* energy to motivate lazy or resistant individuals to get back on task and/or to change destructive behavior. The driving force can also be used to help groups stay together and persevere through the uncomfortable by-products of change. During droughts and economic crises, the Dominant's protective, boundary-setting abilities keep predators at bay and prevent opportunistic herd members from hoarding or hijacking limited resources.

### Benefits of a Mature Human or Animal Dominant

Has a "direct-and-protect" orientation.
Excels at setting boundaries with aggressors.
Challenges predators.
Breaks up fights.
Herds others away from danger.
Motivates lazy or resistant individuals.
Socializes adolescents to use power appropriately.
Directs group members toward common goals.
Protects valuable resources from those who would take advantage.

## Living and Working with Dominants

Until I learned to work effectively with dominant horses, I had no idea how to use this role constructively, let alone how to help naturally dominant humans transform their tempestuous power into a conscious, relationship-*enhancing* force. Due to the nonverbal and emotional dynamics involved, the most effective techniques are difficult to describe and counterintuitive to the average adult, which is why horse-facilitated learning activities offer the most efficient route to mastering this particular role. After all, if you can set boundaries with thousand-pound alpha horses, joyfully direct them to trot around an arena, and invite them to follow you off lead without letting them herd you, it is thereafter much harder for a two-hundred-pound human to intimidate you. Even so, in the equine-facilitated learning field, you have to be very careful whom you study with: Far too many facilitators model an unrefined use of dominance themselves. Some create activities that actually reinforce adolescent, alpha-style hierarchies.

Still, there are some skills that can be translated into words. The following four "power principles" will help you handle aggressive energy with dignity and poise, while forging stronger, mutually supportive relationships with naturally dominant people and animals.

### Power Principle One

*Pay attention to body posture and breathing,*
*using both as nonverbal communication.*

Though the vast majority of dominant humans and animals are completely unconscious of what they're doing, they have a pronounced ability to project their power outward, causing others to yield. From a distance of ten to twenty feet, you can feel a dominant horse pushing as he or she approaches. Even when the body language isn't particularly threatening, this animal's focused, driving energy causes most people to hold their breath, collapse slightly, and take a few steps back. If such a horse is walking behind you, the same force will cause you to hold your breath and arch your back as he or she begins to herd you. Either way, how you respond makes a huge difference in turning this trend around.

Here's the challenge: Yielding causes a Dominant to take more liberties. A horse who successfully invades your space may start pushing you around and playfully grabbing at your clothes. The next thing you know, he or she is ripping your coat off and knocking you to the ground — all in good fun, from the horse's perspective at least.

Tensing up and fighting back, on the other hand, results in a power struggle that can escalate to violence on both sides, resulting in a barrage of flying dust mixed with considerable shouting, swearing, kicking, biting, and rearing. This usually ends in a beating for the horse, serious injuries for the human, or a last-minute leap over the fence.

The alternative to both of these disturbing options sounds simple, but it can be difficult to employ under stress: When a dominant horse approaches, you *will* feel an initial impulse to hold your breath, collapse or arch your back, and either move away or fight back. But you can turn these instinctual reactions around by *breathing deeply and standing your ground with a slightly rounded, aligned spine, neither leaning forward nor bracing back*. This communicates a centered confidence that neither attacks nor defers to the Dominant's controlling, potentially aggressive intent.

With humans, this posture, and the attitude behind it, are in themselves unexpectedly effective. After all, bosses and colleagues aren't likely to physically push you around. They're usually sitting at desks or conference tables.

In setting boundaries with horses, however, it's helpful to use a whip as an extension of your arm. This allows you to claim your space without touching the animal. That is, you don't hit the horse with the whip, but you wave the whip in front of you to keep the horse from stepping too close. If, instead of using a whip or stick, you make physical contact by holding up your hand, the horse experiences this as successfully stepping into your space. He or she *is* touching you after all. If you push against an adolescent dominant horse in such close proximity, he or she is likely to reach down and bite you, especially if the horse reads this pushing sensation as a challenge.

Here's the counterintuitive part, especially in working with Dominants: No matter how intensely they try to invade your space, you must give them *immediate positive feedback* the split second they back off. When horses make the slightest effort to yield to your request for space, you give them immediate positive feedback by putting the whip in a neutral position, breathing, and relaxing. When human Dominants back off, you give them immediate positive feedback by relaxing, making brief, friendly eye contact, and getting back on task.

Why do you do this? Anyone who overemphasizes the Dominant

role is used to feeling a great deal of frustration, fear, anger, helplessness, and animosity from coworkers and family members. By the time most people finally stand their ground with a dominant colleague, boss, spouse, or child, they have *had it*, and they are likely to rage at this individual, ostracize the person, or leave him or her — sometimes all three in close succession. As a result, some Dominants never learn the *benefits* of respecting others. They only know that people either defer to them or explode and leave.

It's an incredible, potentially transformational gift to set a boundary with a Dominant, methodically and unemotionally, *long before you feel rage*. In meeting a person's or horse's aggressive energy with a centered, confident presence, offering immediate positive feedback when the Dominant backs off, you make it clear that you're capable of standing your ground without trying to intimidate, humiliate, or push the other around. In the process, you model an approach to power that gives everyone hope.

## Power Principle Two

*Distinguish between setting boundaries and motivating others, using the assertiveness formula to employ power as needed.*

In one of my favorite photos of the Fulani pastoralist lifestyle, a single male herder, surrounded by a dozen cows and bulls, drives these animals across a rushing river while maintaining a three-foot "safety zone" around his own body. Here he's employing dominance to simultaneously direct the group toward the opposite shore *and* set a boundary that keeps the animals from inadvertently kicking him, pushing him under water, or skewering him with their massive horns. Clearly, it's an advanced move. Still, this dramatic image masterfully illustrates the benefits of using dominant energy to (1) *claim your own space* and (2) *motivate others to perform a specific goal*.

In working with those who overemphasize dominance, however, it's initially helpful to separate these two activities so that the difference between them becomes apparent. Dominants are less likely to misuse power when they learn to respect others' space. From there, it's much easier to show them how to motivate people using a controlled and thoughtful form of assertiveness (in lieu of pushing others around aggressively).

When setting a boundary, you want to make it obvious that you're not ordering someone else around; you're simply claiming the physical or emotional space you need to feel safe, respected, *and therefore connected* to the individual you're interacting with. Motivating someone, on the other hand, involves using assertiveness to influence behavior, often by directing him or her to take action toward a specific goal. Both activities involve a skillful use of power. You can avoid adding aggression, shame, blame, and resentment to these actions by using a formula that helps anyone employ the Dominant's divisive and driving forms of energy in a humane, controlled manner:

Assertiveness = Commitment + Crescendo
+ Immediate Positive Feedback

Because dominant horses and humans alike have strong opinions and an urge to control others' behavior, you must be absolutely committed to holding your ground with them. If you're the least bit wishy-washy about claiming your space, they will sense this and use it to their advantage.

In adolescent alphas, the inclination to push boundaries and take over is so instinctual that you cannot rely on words or logic to gain cooperation. You must back up an already-strong commitment with real power. This is where the *crescendo* comes in. People who are inexperienced or afraid to use power often try to beg, guilt-trip, or insult a Dominant into respecting them. This is like throwing gas on a fire. People who overemphasize this role *rarely* respond to shaming language by collapsing and backing off. This tactic actually seems to turn an initially unemotional impulse to dominate into a mission fueled by rage. Progressively "dialing up" your power is the only way to show a Dominant that *you have power* and *know how to use it without malice* to enhance relationships, rather than dominate or victimize others.

A crescendo is a gradual increase in volume or energy that does not back down or release pressure until it reaches its fulfillment. Musicians learn to do this for expressive, purely aesthetic reasons. Most people, however, don't develop this important skill, though there are many good reasons to use it daily in all kinds of contexts.

To employ the crescendo, it's helpful to imagine that you have a power dial in your solar plexus that you can use to turn the intensity up or down as needed. When setting boundaries with Dominants, you may have to take the power up to an 8 or 9 before they back off, especially if they're accustomed to intimidating others into submission. However, you must show them that you're in complete mastery of this power by dialing the volume up progressively. Start at 1 or 2 and progress through 3, 4, 5, 6, and so on, offering immediate positive feedback the moment they show respect.

The same assertiveness formula applies to motivating others. If you're asking a horse to trot around the arena, for instance, a gentle horse is likely to pick up speed if you gently shake a rope, wave a whip, or use hand gestures (which equals a 1 or 2 on the power dial). However, a dominant horse will initially *refuse to move* as a classic power play. Remember, the alpha moves others around all day, but he or she *never* moves for fellow herd members.

For example, I often invite clients who want to practice advanced assertiveness skills to work with my stallion Merlin's three proud yet reasonably well-socialized sons, Spirit, Indigo Moon, and Orion. I can even accommodate different skill levels with this little herd. Spirit is highly dominant and can be overtly intimidating; Indigo Moon is slightly less challenging. Their much more congenial younger brother, Orion, is also strong willed, though much more polite about it. All three will initially refuse to budge when a new student tries to direct one of them to walk and then trot around the arena.

Many people initially attempt to move these horses by casually pointing to the rail and then waving a hand while making clucking noises. At this point, even Orion is likely to make an exaggerated, almost comical attempt to ignore the student — looking *away* as if the person is less interesting than the nearest tree and no more irritating than a fly. With a bit of encouragement, the client invariably picks up the whip and shakes it limply, unenthusiastically, whereupon Orion in particular will actually lean *backward*, planting his rear feet even more firmly in place.

The next tactic usually involves the person's willingness to wave the whip rhythmically at a 3 or 4 on the dial. This, however, keeps the energy at the same level. When a human suspends the crescendo — as in 1, 2, 3, 4, 4, 4, 4 — dominant horses adjust and "4" becomes the new "1."

Finally, after further coaching, the client will succeed at progressively dialing the power up to a 5, 6, and 7 by increasing the speed and intensity of how he or she waves the whip, moving closer to the horse and becoming more demonstrative. As the client approaches 10, he or she perhaps even cracks the whip (in the air, not touching the horse) and shouts enthusiastically.

As an aside, regardless of how much power is needed, the whip must never be used in anger to hurt or punish the horse, in the same way that power must never be used to hurt or punish those we wish to influence. Even if we have to defend ourselves from an aggressive attack, we must give the person or horse immediate positive feedback when he or she backs off. Then, if necessary, we can institute fair and thoughtful consequences that hold offenders accountable for violent misbehavior.

Because the student's first request for Orion to walk around the arena is met with the Dominant's challenge of refusing to move, the client is usually astonished that he or she has to dial up to an 8 or even 9 before the horse finally concedes to saunter off in the most casual way. But the client usually finds the next interaction even more surprising. Once Orion sees that the student is *committed* to moving him, and capable of employing the *crescendo* followed by *immediate positive feedback* (in the form of putting the whip in a neutral position while praising the horse), the tall and lanky black gelding is likely to trot at 4 or 5 on the dial when the next request is made.

By passing Orion's test — by using higher levels of power without apology or malice — the student thereafter gains the horse's cooperation with more subtle forms of assertiveness.

In motivating resistant employees, coworkers, and family members, the same formula applies, though using a whip is not likely to win anyone over. Instead, the crescendo involves a progression of actions that increase power and influence while directing someone to carry out a task. Here, the "power dial" might proceed like this: (1) emailing to check in or remind the person of a deadline; (2) texting with a bit more urgent or assertive language; (3) calling the person if there's no response; (4) stopping by the person's office to check in on progress; (5) calling a formal meeting with the person in your office; (6) engaging a more serious yet private "difficult conversation"; (7) formally writing a warning, and so on through levels 8, 9, and 10, which might culminate in dismissal.

At any time during this sequence, it's important to offer immediate positive feedback when the person cooperates, in the form of relaxed, gently approving eye contact and a professional statement like "looks good, we're making some progress here." Immediate positive feedback also involves your ability to move forward with a congenial attitude, without holding a grudge, even if you have to dial up higher than you think you should.

These days, far too many supervisors tend to text and text and text again, then get frustrated and explode. This is like trying to move Orion by limply waving the whip for five minutes, then suddenly racing toward the horse, cracking the whip, and shouting obscenities — or what would feel like 2, 2, 2, 2, 10!!!! If you stay at a 2 and then suddenly blast your power above an 8, even a dominant person will think you're hysterical or unnecessarily abusive. Dialing your power up progressively without adding rage and insults to the mix allows you to engage the upper range of intensity, if necessary, in a way that feels clean, fair, and controlled.

As with Orion, this formula, when used mindfully and masterfully, creates greater *cooperation* and *self-motivation* in others over time, freeing leaders up for other pursuits.

Why must we distinguish between boundary setting and assertiveness? There are three reasons actually: (1) The goals are very different. (2) The timing and the positive feedback are different. (3) The emotions that arise are different.

First of all, in setting a boundary, you're claiming the space, time, or consideration *you* need to be effective, not directing someone else's behavior. In the case of setting boundaries with resources, such as money or property, you're protecting what you already have, not trying to acquire more. The split second someone backs off, you reward him or her with relaxed, appreciative engagement before getting back on task. When someone repeatedly or aggressively steps over your boundaries, you will feel anger.

When you're motivating someone else to perform a goal, you're often pushing *his or her* boundaries for a specific purpose, sometimes asking the person to step outside his or her comfort zone, sacrifice resources, or compromise his or her need for personal space, time, and so on. Usually, this is in order to serve the needs of the organization, family, or culture at large. Standard positive feedback involves some kind of reward or recognition when the goal is completed. But on more complex, long-term projects, it's helpful to engage immediate positive feedback for efforts to get started, endure, and troubleshoot. This means that as the motivator, you're adding enthusiasm, appreciation, and perhaps additional training along the way.

In fact, unless an already-motivated person is taking a break, the "relaxed connection" feedback used in boundary setting is counterproductive. For instance, in motivating a horse to move from a walk to a trot, appreciation must be communicated when the horse makes the transition *without* dropping the energy level, or the horse will fall back into a walk. With a person who's reluctant to perform a necessary yet boring, tedious task, he or she doesn't need any excuse to relax and take a break; this person needs to be energized, probably requiring a more assertive crescendo to get started, boosted by enthusiasm and even a bit of humor from you to lighten the load.

In the context of assertiveness/motivation, if someone drops the ball or needs constant attention to stay on task, you will feel frustrated because you've "hit the wall" in getting the person to do his or her job in general or take specific action on a previously agreed upon goal.

## Power Principle Three

*Do not take dominance games personally.*

Once again, this is counterintuitive. It's natural to feel insulted or even betrayed by a Dominant's willful behavior, public challenges, and overt or covert refusals to cooperate. Most unnerving, of course, is that intense, oddly instinctual strategy of attacking others for little or no reason.

In working with people who overemphasize the Dominant role, however, it's important to realize that *the power plays are endless.* If you understand the primal roots of this behavior, at least you won't be shocked by it. As a result, you'll be much more likely to remain thoughtful in these situations and minimize the damage.

An accomplished supervisor can modulate the behavior of dominant staff members, but unbalanced alphas will unleash the same predictable forms of mischief on others when the boss leaves the room. These unproductive, often-hurtful, yet still-predictable games are unlikely to fade in any organization or family until naturally dominant individuals learn how to use the strengths of this role in balance with the skills endemic to the other roles. Even with skillful coaching, it can take months or even years for such people to transform their fiery instinctual impulses into a mature, refined, fully conscious source of power.

In the meantime, it's important to change your own response to the Dominant's more outlandish behavior. If an alpha-style boss jumps all over you for some minor misunderstanding, there's no need to spend a single sleepless night wondering why he or she doesn't respect you. Resist the urge to spiral down into the all-too-common thought loop:

"I've been so good to this person, so loyal and helpful, and then what happens? My boss turns around and insults me in front of the entire staff."

With mal-socialized Dominants, *it's not about you.* They'll target someone else for similar treatment next week. In doing so, they'll continue to lose trust and alienate *themselves* from the group — until they're willing to alter the destructive by-products of what is potentially an incredible talent for directing and protecting others.

Here's another odd feature of dominant behavior that confuses people to no end. Let's say a colleague named Henry rakes you over the coals for an easily correctable, unintentional mistake. You might think he's at war with you for some indecipherable reason, or maybe he just plain doesn't like you. Then a few days later, he vehemently defends you when someone from another department questions your judgment. From a Dominant's perspective, this makes perfect sense. Henry is doing what Dominants do well: protecting a member of his herd. However, he also reserves the right to launch unexpected attacks on those same herd members to keep them in line.

I experienced something very much like this at an equestrian conference a few years back. One of the clinicians, whom I'll call "Jake," is a talented, quite famous horse trainer. He is an admittedly alpha-style leader, and he wasn't shy about challenging me on several occasions during informal gatherings and conversations. Then, during a large exhibition, a member of the audience decided it would be fun to try to fluster and possibly discredit me. The spectator actually interrupted my presentation and tried to hijack it by questioning a minor feature of what I was demonstrating.

This sort of thing rarely happens, but when it does, I've learned how to turn a challenge into a good-natured opportunity for everyone, including me, to learn something new. At least I can most of the time, since I sincerely enjoy debating subjects I care about.

Still, before I could fully address this person's comments, Jake jumped up from his chair, stepped in front as if shielding me from a possible attack, and defended my approach with gusto. I was shocked.

But from what I now know about the instinctual characteristics of Dominants, the tendency to alternately provoke and protect people is both common and predictable.

## Power Principle Four

*Resist the temptation to enlist a Dominant to compensate
for others' avoidance of this role. Instead, coach all staff
in the appropriate use of power.*

Many people abdicate the Dominant role because they're uncomfortable with power. As I described earlier, this was certainly my inclination early in my career. When I was promoted to program director of a radio station, I relied on the station manager to step in when my congenial, inspirational approach wasn't strong enough to handle conflicts between staff members and get uncooperative employees back on track.

However, when I started my own business, this unbalanced leadership style became a liability, and I truly learned what kind of trouble I could get into if I didn't employ the strengths of the Dominant role. I wanted everybody to get along. I wanted people to be self-motivated and to employ all the wonderful emotional and social intelligence tools we were learning from the horses. But staff members would have conflicts. Because I refused to step in assertively soon enough, the animosity between two people sometimes escalated beyond a point of no return, as people said things they couldn't take back. Factions emerged as staff members took sides. This created an increasingly toxic working environment. Finally, I had to let certain people go. In effect, by refusing to use dominance, I eventually had to perform the predatory act of firing an otherwise talented staff member.

Another classic dilemma ensues when a leader can't motivate resistant employees. Sometimes this is related to the "refusal to move" power play enacted by a naturally dominant staff member. Just as often, the lack of motivation stems from the fact that we all encounter tedious parts of our jobs — boring or challenging functions that we'd rather avoid. If a kind-hearted boss doesn't know how to get someone back on task, the effect on other staff members is significant. Some people pick up the slack. Others become more complacent. Over time, frustration and resentment rise as efficiency and responsibility fall.

A common fix involves hiring a dominant middle manager. However, because everyone relies on this person to be the disciplinarian, the entire organization actually supports him or her in overemphasizing the role. This, in turn, encourages the shadow side of the Dominant to become more pronounced. Over time, the Dominant will increasingly be portrayed as a Neanderthal, an egotistical maniac, or simply "the bad guy."

People who *overidentify* with the Leader, Sentinel, or Nurturer/ Companion roles invariably neglect to develop the skills associated with the Dominant role. As a result, they're much more likely to enter into an unholy alliance with a dominant monster they create. Someone naturally talented in the divisive energy that can break up fights and the driving energy that can break through resistance is susceptible to becoming a scapegoat for the naïve, irresponsible behavior of those who abdicate this role. People who refuse to *use* dominance *need* Dominants to do their dirty work for them. And while people may appreciate the function Dominants perform, they also love to hate them.

# CHAPTER FOUR

# Discover and Inspire:
# Leadership through Relationship

## *Role: Leader*

Several years ago, I adopted three young mares from a local horse rescue. Leyla, a brown-and-white paint with striking blue eyes, walked right up to me the day we met, while Brandi, a chestnut with a flaxen mane and tail, watched from a safe distance. Feisty little Savannah — a delicate, spirited buckskin — also kept her distance, though her gaze seemed more suspicious than shy.

When bringing new horses onto the property, I always keep them separate for a couple of weeks to make sure they aren't carrying any communicable diseases. But since Leyla, Brandi, and Savannah had already been living together with a large group of mares at the Equine Voices rescue center, I turned them out together in a half-acre corral away from the rest of my herd. Within a matter of weeks, I couldn't believe my good fortune. In observing the already well-established dynamics of this trio, I realized that I had somehow managed to acquire a mini-herd whose members exemplified the differences between the Leader, the Dominant, and the Nurturer/Companion, with all three trading the Sentinel role as needed.

These mares were so closely bonded, so in sync with one another, that my staff and I began calling them the "Spice Girls." Like the British band, each member was beautiful in her own unique way. The group also proved to be unusually resistant to letting other horses into their "girl-power" clique.

By far the smallest of the three, Savannah was the alpha. At dinnertime, the caramel-colored beauty would not only strut toward the feeder of her choice, she would chase Brandi and Leyla away from their hay at various points during the meal. Sometimes Savannah would let them eat with her, but it was clearly a privilege that could be revoked on a whim. True to her dominant personality, the buckskin would also lunge at Brandi or Leyla at other times of the day for no apparent reason.

Savannah was by far the most insecure in dealing with change and the most committed in controlling the others' behavior. For instance, if I took Brandi or Leyla out for training, Savannah would race back and forth, calling out for ten or fifteen minutes, unable to relax until her herd was back together. When it was Savannah's turn to leave, the other mares seemed to appreciate the break, whinnying a few times before settling down to rest or eat in peace. Still, I appreciated Savannah's commitment to protecting the mares. If one of my other horses wandered near the Spice Girls' corral, Savannah would drive Brandi and Leyla toward the center and then rush back over to chase the interloper away. As a result, I never had to worry about any of these mares getting hurt playing with other horses over the fence.

The outlandish behavior of dominant horses is hard to miss, and Savannah was no exception. However, herd leaders are much more difficult to spot. Among young horses, those with an aptitude for this role rarely show their talent until a novel situation arises.

One day, I asked a staff member to stack some flashy green metal corral panels in the Spice Girls' wire-fenced compound. I wanted to set up a small arena and some holding pens in this large enclosure so that the trio could begin working with clients in a familiar space. This way, these still-young mares would feel more secure and thus more open to working with new people.

As expected, Savannah swiftly drove her herd away from this strange new feature of their environment. Within minutes, however,

Leyla broke away and began to approach the shiny new panels, her initial caution quickly giving way to curiosity and finally comfort. Soon Brandi and Savannah were sniffing the "green monster" as well.

That evening, however, the buckskin Savannah made it a point to repeatedly chase Leyla away from her hay. From the Dominant's point of view, this made perfect sense. Earlier that day, Brandi had left Savannah to follow Leyla, whose poise and interest in something that had clearly unnerved the alpha gave Brandi new confidence. Soon after, Savannah also found herself trailing along behind Leyla.

Once everything seemed safe and normal again, however, the buckskin was noticeably irked, as if she felt threatened by Leyla's ability to take on a leadership role. For a good thirty minutes, Savannah tried to put Leyla back in her place by lunging at her whenever she took a step toward food or water.

Then Brandi gently intervened, showing, in the process, her own talent for the Nurturer/Companion role. Over the course of an hour, I watched the soulful chestnut groom Savannah and Leyla separately, no doubt releasing a hefty dose of oxytocin in them all, creating a "calm-and-connect" response that softened the buckskin's demeanor. Eventually, Brandi succeeded in facilitating a mutual grooming session with all three mares in close contact. As the sun set over this revealing incident, the Spice Girls were in harmony once again.

Throughout that first summer, I watched the same pattern unfold under similar circumstances. For the most part — when Savannah wasn't playing dominance games — the Spice Girls engaged in consensual leadership: Decisions were made through a kind of meandering group consciousness, similar to the way that experienced shepherds merge with their flocks and sometimes can't tell whose idea it was to move in a certain direction. But this peaceful pastoral dynamic suddenly changed when something truly novel occurred. Then the Dominant would drive her little herd away from possible danger, the Leader would break away from the alpha to investigate, and the others would eventually follow.

Over time, as all the mares matured, Savannah grew to appreciate

Leyla's judgment and became less likely to attack the blue-eyed mare in the aftermath of unusual situations. What's more, the Spice Girls' human caretakers learned how to leverage the talents of the various group members. Whenever we had to move the horses, for instance, things went much smoother if we led Leyla into a new setting first, with Brandi in the middle and Savannah bringing up the rear.

> ## Characteristics of a Young Human or Animal Leader
>
> Is attracted to novel situations.
>
> Explores the possible benefits of new or unusual environmental features, relationships, and processes that others ignore or actively avoid.
>
> Exhibits curiosity and confidence that others find contagious.

## A Leader in the Making

Among horses and other large herbivores, certain individuals exhibit poise in the midst of change and even outright attraction to anything new in the landscape. While other herd members avoid the unfamiliar, a leader in the making will employ appropriate yet short-lived caution, slowly moving toward the unconventional object with a confidence and curiosity others find contagious. Without any overt ambition, these mavericks become leaders because others *choose* to follow them.

While both the Leader and the Dominant employ active influence, the two roles are polar opposites in the execution of their power. The alpha uses a directive, *pushing* energy, driving others toward or away from something. A consummate protector, the Dominant tends to be skeptical of anything new and easily escalates to intimidation in the face of danger or resistance.

The Leader, on the other hand, radiates a compelling, *pulling* energy, drawing others forward, motivating the herd through inspiration and optimism, while sometimes taking risks to explore possibilities that others might never consider.

Unlike Dominants, who sometimes stir up trouble to gain influence, Leaders *conserve energy for true emergencies*. They tend to avoid interpersonal dramas and power plays in favor of examining some intriguing feature of the environment. While young horses like Leyla are susceptible to attacks from an adolescent Dominant like Savannah, mature herd Leaders become skilled at setting effective boundaries with aggressors — without trying to control others' behavior.

Over time, horses gifted in this role add considerable life experience to the mix, gaining respect from mature Dominants in the process. Herd members rely on the Leader's knowledge, courage, and judgment to guide them toward greener pastures and help them temper survival instincts to explore unconventional opportunities. In this respect, a Leader's ability to assess the intentions of predators, herd members, and other species at a distance is crucial — or such an adventurous animal would be quickly taken out of the gene pool.

### Characteristics of a Mature Human or Animal Leader

Exhibits heightened knowledge of terrain, food and water sources, and predators.

Calms and focuses others in tense or novel situations.

Does not get involved in petty herd dramas.

Sets effective boundaries with aggressors and Dominants and then goes "back to grazing."

## Toward the Dream

Human Leaders add creativity and, in some cases, advanced communication skills to the mix, resulting in some additional benefits and challenges. Like their equine counterparts, people with a talent for this role draw attention to *opportunities* in unfamiliar settings, as opposed to focusing on potential dangers. But two-legged Leaders take this impulse one colossal step further — they *envision* and *manifest* future possibilities. It is precisely during the manifestation phase that their leadership abilities emerge. Successfully rallying others to the cause is only the first step in managing the many challenges staff or constituents will face along the way.

A great Leader has the focus and endurance to motivate others through the uncomfortable realities of change. An immature human Leader is likely to emerge with a lofty vision that attracts others while lacking the multifaceted skills needed to keep people on task and negotiate the many technical and interpersonal difficulties that arise.

Less susceptible to tradition and public opinion, people with a talent for this role show remarkable courage for investigation and experimentation. While some innovators seem shy in conventional social settings, they're not easily controlled, mostly because safety achieved through conformity is anathema to them. They would rather become loners than relinquish their natural curiosity. And when a vision takes hold of them, they exhibit a remarkable tenacity. While other "herd members" fear change and feel intense embarrassment in making mistakes, visionary Leaders in particular exhibit a high tolerance for vulnerability and rebound quickly from failure, using just about any block or blunder as course-correcting information.

In challenging situations, Leaders seek innovative solutions as their Dominant counterparts try to enforce the status quo, sometimes resulting in power struggles that keep everyone in limbo. For this reason, great Leaders must have proficiency in the other roles to address the concerns of followers, stand up to dominant factions, and drive complacent herd members toward a dream that may have to be adapted to the needs of the community. Otherwise, even the simplest, well-intentioned vision may die on the vine.

## Advanced Benefits of a Human Leader

Exhibits exceptional visionary qualities.
Calms and focuses large populations during a crisis.
Motivates through inspiration.
Troubleshoots with innovative solutions.

## The Visionary's Dilemma

People who overemphasize this role face predictable challenges that sometimes result in their failure to complete worthwhile projects. Immature Leaders fixate on serving the vision, and they expect everyone else to do the same. Great Leaders refine and humanize the goal by staying in touch with those they lead.

A visionary with a socially conscious agenda, for instance, might start a nonprofit that just about anyone would get behind. Yet if this person lacks the interpersonal and assertiveness skills associated with the Nurturer/Companion and Dominant roles, he or she is likely to alienate some staff members while letting others get away with all kinds of unproductive behavior — even as the Leader continues to inspire everyone with a laudable, save-the-world plan.

People who show a marked talent for this role must modulate their impatience with the social dramas that others find so engrossing. When employees engage in power plays, for instance, an unbalanced Leader will either ignore the conflict or urge everyone to "focus on the big picture." A promising nonprofit's goal might be to feed the hungry, which makes daily office politics look minor in comparison, but interpersonal difficulties among key staff members can prevent the entire organization from fulfilling its mission. For this reason alone, a Leader must learn to intervene early enough and decisively enough to change unproductive behavior.

Artistic fields are particularly susceptible to hiring immature Leaders with a compelling vision. In the 2014 documentary film *Lost Soul: The Doomed Journey of Richard Stanley's Island of Dr. Moreau*, the filmmakers capture a sweet, creative, optimistic writer-director enacting all the classic challenges of someone who overemphasizes the Leader role.

After previous success in creating campy horror films that gained a cult following, Richard Stanley was given the chance to develop a mainstream Hollywood movie based on one of his favorite books. Over time, however, he proved incapable of juggling the myriad organizational details, special interests, and massive egos involved. While most Leaders have access to at least some of the strengths of one or two other roles, Stanley's sometimes-amusing, sometimes-heartbreaking story offers a dramatic case study of a man who truly lacked proficiency in the Sentinel, Nurturer/Companion, Dominant, and Predator roles. With little more than an intriguing vision and the nerve to manifest it, Stanley's failure is almost guaranteed, despite a multi-million-dollar budget and a cast of legendary actors.

### Challenges of a Human Leader

Can lose touch with others, appearing aloof or self-absorbed.
Sometimes gets so far out in front of the group that others can't follow.
Seems unsympathetic or easily frustrated by interpersonal dramas.
Can take on too much responsibility due to difficulty delegating tasks.

## Washington's Barn: Great Leadership in Action

In contrast, it's helpful to analyze the abilities of a truly gifted, well-balanced Leader in action. One of the most striking examples involves a relatively mundane incident in George Washington's life. As president of the United States, Washington was considered one of the most powerful men in the world. But he found splitting time between the new government center in Philadelphia and his beloved Virginia farm rife with challenges.

While dealing with a contentious Congress, Washington often received letters outlining troubles at home. After fighting the unexpectedly long Revolutionary War *as a volunteer*, the former general considered agricultural matters urgent, as he supported himself primarily through plantation-generated income. But in the late-1700s, his profit margins were compromised by several factors: Widely accepted methods of threshing wheat, his main cash crop, were incredibly inefficient. Nighttime bandits were stealing grain. And whenever Washington left the property for extended periods, Mount Vernon's workers became complacent, sometimes neglecting to follow his explicit instructions.

As Alan and Donna Jean Fusonie reveal in *George Washington: Pioneer Farmer*, "His diary entries reflect his frustration over the uncontrollable elements of weather, disease, and, at times, reluctant slave labor." While Washington had no problem employing the Dominant role, the need to micromanage enslaved workers was draining personally, financially, and morally, even when he was able to oversee the farm in person.

After the Revolutionary War, America remained immersed in a plantation system that depended on slavery, but Washington himself found that his ability to objectify others, no matter what their race or culture, had seriously eroded. He had come to believe that one day slavery would be eradicated, though he considered this unrealistic in his own time.

As a result of this increasing awareness and compassion, Washington refused to callously sell off the family members of his own slaves. Over time, of course, this meant that he was feeding and clothing more people than he needed for labor, and he was losing money in the process. He also came to realize that slavery itself was not an efficient business model: People forced to work against their will would only ever do the bare minimum, even under relentless supervision. On

Washington's farm, the issue of how to motivate his workers came to a head over threshing wheat. But rather than solve the matter using violent intimidation — a then-common method that was legally available to any slave owner — Washington chose an inventive approach.

As the Fusonies report in their book on the president's pioneering agricultural innovations:

> Two customary methods of separating — or threshing — the wheat were available to Washington. Striking the wheat with a wooden instrument called a flail was commonly performed by laborers, free and slave, on large wooden floors centered in rectangular barns. The force of the hand-held flail knocked loose the grain. Another, ancient method was known as treading. This involved laying the wheat outdoors in a larger circle or oval and driving horses atop the wheat, their stamping hooves performing the same task as the flails.

The latter method was less efficient and incredibly unsanitary, as the wheat would be ground into dirt, urine, manure, and sometimes mud during a particularly stormy harvest season. Plus, laborers had to work under the hot sun or pouring rain to gather and clean the wheat, hopefully before nightfall when people were inclined to steal whatever was left outside. So Washington spent two years building a hundred-foot-long, brick threshing barn where slaves could flail the wheat out of the sun and rain and lock their efforts up at the end of the day.

Visitors often admired the impressively crafted barn, but the people who were supposed to use it did *not* appreciate it. "Because of Washington's extended absences from home during the presidency, his best plans often went awry," the Fusonies emphasize. In a 1793 letter to a friend, the president expressed considerable disappointment that despite having

> one of the most convenient Barns in this, or perhaps any other Country, where 30 hands may with great ease be employed in threshing...notwithstanding, when I came home...I found a treading yard not 30 feet from the Barn door, the Wheat again

brought out of the Barn and horses treading it out in an open exposure liable to the vicissitudes of weather.

You can well imagine what Washington was thinking, probably for days: "I'm the president of the United States, for God's sake! I defeated the British with the most incredible odds against me. I spent *huge* amounts of money to build this state-of-the-art threshing barn, and I can't get my slaves, or the staff that oversees them, to use it unless I'm standing over all of them with a whip!"

Yet even with all the other pressures he was under, history doesn't record Washington throwing a well-deserved tantrum. Instead, he did something much more outrageous. He took *everyone's* concerns into consideration and drew up some new plans, creating a sophisticated multilevel building that combined the strengths of a threshing barn *and* a treading yard.

In what looked like an indoor round pen, the second floor of this sixteen-sided structure featured a circular track on a wood floor with thin slats between each board. To thresh wheat, a few workers would lay wheat stalks on the track, and then handlers would lead a couple of horses up a ramp and close the barn door. Then, a single trainer would stand in the center and exercise the animals at a trot. As the horses treaded over the wheat, the grain would slip through the slats onto a clean, dry surface below. This lower floor could easily be secured with a padlock, whether or not workers had time to bag the grain before sunset.

In July 2011, *Forbes* cited Washington's threshing barn as one of "The Five Best Inventions of the Founding Fathers." Writer Alex Knapp didn't mention the drama that inspired Washington to create this unique structure, but the author did emphasize the following:

> The horses were made to continually run so that they wouldn't urinate or defecate on the grain, and there were gaps in the floor that the treaded grain would come out of for easy collection. It was a simple, but very practical invention. And personally,

anything that reduces the amount of fecal matter in food is, in my mind, a good invention.

Still, the truly innovative aspects of this story far transcend the agricultural benefits. Here we see that Washington — a general capable of employing the Dominant and Predator roles when necessary — clearly preferred a visionary leadership role when push came to shove. But even this role was seasoned with the thoughtful observational capabilities of a Sentinel and the empathy of a Nurturer/Companion. By taking the perspectives and the needs of his workers into consideration, Washington moved beyond his initial frustration with their lack of acceptance of the traditional rectangular threshing barn he'd built. At the same time, he addressed his own priorities to create a clean, efficient, secure solution to a challenge that farmers had been grappling with for millennia.

# CHAPTER FIVE

# Support and Connect:
# The Power of Companionship

## *Role: Nurturer / Companion*

When a well-known computer software company hired Greg Reid, MS, to solve some staff-related difficulties, the business consultant, organizational psychologist, and sociometrist was asked to address two confounding, oddly complementary situations. One group, known informally as "the curmudgeons," or sometimes "the negative stars," consisted of high-performing, socially challenged employees. They tended to isolate themselves at work and leave right at five o'clock, but their productivity was on target.

Then there was "Melanie," a socially gifted programmer with the opposite problem.

"Everyone really likes Melanie, but her productivity is low," the head of human resources told Greg. "We're at our wit's end on this one. If we can't figure out how to help her, we're going to have to let her go."

Through interviews and testing, Greg studied the company's interpersonal dynamics, paying special attention to communication flow. What he found was astonishing.

"When most people went on vacation, there was about a 5 percent drop in productivity due to each individual's absence," he told me during a phone interview. "But when this one woman left the office for an extended period, the difference was glaring. Every time she took a vacation, there was up to a *36 percent drop in company productivity across the board*."

It turned out that Melanie, an intelligent, energetic, thirty-year-old employee, didn't have *time* to do her own job because she was busy performing a much more important function: facilitating connection between multiple departments. "She was the kind of person who could speak 'geek' and regular English," Greg laughed, only partially joking. "As a result, she was able to break through and communicate with 'the negative stars.' She would take that extra-long lunch and talk to everyone." In the process, Melanie became the "go-to" person for all kinds of information. And when she wasn't around, the company suffered.

Luckily, Greg's discoveries led to some thoughtful reorganization. Management shifted her goals, reducing expectations for programming while officially recognizing her facilitator role. A year later, they moved her into a position as project leader.

## The Age of Nurture?

Despite statistics on the importance of emotional and social intelligence in the workplace, many people are marginalized for the same reason Melanie was almost let go. Bottom-line sales figures and other productivity measures do not recognize the contributions of those who support *process*: all those behind-the-scenes functions that enhance communication between individuals and facilitate collaboration between departments that might otherwise ignore or compete with one another.

Among herbivores and carnivores, some herd or pack members also prove to be gifted connectors. Recall the "Spice Girls" from chapter 4: Brandi was able to moderate conflict between Savannah and Leyla by reaching out to each individual separately, and she ultimately succeeded in bringing them back together through the oxytocin-boosting activity of mutual grooming. Like Melanie, who could speak "geek" and "regular English," the chestnut mare proved equally adept at relating to the herd Dominant and the herd Leader, even when those two clashed due to differences in priorities, talents, and "working style."

In conquest-oriented cultures, however, caring, empathetic behavior is seen as a weakness, especially in professional settings. For thousands of years, the Nurturer/Companion role was relegated to "women's work" and dismissed as an extracurricular activity that men might enjoy with their families or perhaps explore one day a week in church if they were so inclined.

The tide began to turn in the late-twentieth and early-twenty-first centuries. Researchers like Daniel Goleman, and journalists writing for the *Harvard Business Review*, *Entrepreneur*, and other respected periodicals, began chronicling a shift away from stoic, autocratic, intensely hierarchical leadership practices. *Inc.* magazine's Leigh Buchanan went so far as to cite JetBlue, Whole Foods, and Zappo's executives as representatives of an emerging Age of Nurture.

In practice, the mainstream lags far behind. As Melanie's story illustrates, those with a talent for the Nurturer/Companion role continue to be misunderstood and devalued in competitive business, educational, and political settings.

## Characteristics of a Human or Animal Nurturer/Companion

Monitors and promotes well-being in individuals and in the group.

Strives to make others feel comfortable.

Facilitates connections between those who might otherwise avoid contact.

Promotes the oxytocin response, the "glue" that holds the herd and tribe together (see pages 42–44).

When more extroverted, can socialize with an unusually wide range of individuals.

When more introverted, can be an invaluable source of loyalty and support to a smaller circle of family, herd, and/or team members.

## An Unexpected Strength

Organizational development specialist Juli Lynch, PhD, whose expertise was instrumental in creating the Master Herder Professional Assessment for this book, travels the country as an executive coach and business consultant. A valued colleague of mine, she also employs the Eponaquest approach to equine-facilitated learning and has found the Master Herder model useful in corporate trainings.

As we were developing the assessment, Juli decided to use an early version at a medium-size community bank in west Texas. After taking the test, the bank's leadership team learned which of the five roles each member tended to emphasize or avoid, leading to a lively conversation. Even so, "Nick," a branch president, seemed preoccupied as he considered the results of his profile. Moments later he interrupted the discussion.

"I think I did the assessment wrong," he announced. "I need to do it over again."

"Why is that?" Juli asked.

"I have a pretty high score on the Nurturer/Companion," he said stoically. Juli later discovered that he actually scored the *highest* in this area, a fact he didn't initially admit to the group.

Juli remembers, "This guy stood at about six-foot-three, and anyone could tell that he was ex-military. He was clean shaven, with a buzz haircut. He wore an overly starched and overly pressed collared shirt with perfectly ironed seams along the arms. His eyes were a steel gray, and his face had that chiseled look of a courtyard statue."

Nick stared unflinchingly at Juli, communicating a silent challenge. "At the same time," she says, "I noticed his team passing sideways glances at one another — little smirkish smiles crossing their faces as their eyes widened with surprise and a hint of humor."

"Well," she responded to Nick, "you are welcome to take the assessment again, but tell me why you think that score is incorrect?"

The words burst out of his mouth: "I'm not a touchy-feely type, okay?"

The entire room erupted into laughter.

"*What?*" he exclaimed, turning toward his colleagues. "Why are y'all laughing? You think I'm touchy-feely?"

"Well, Mr. Retired Marine," one of the women replied, "you may think you are a tough guy, but I see you as a really caring guy — especially when one of us needs a little lovin'."

This resulted in a stream of playful, good-natured comments.

"You are a softy, come on, admit it," cajoled another member of his all-women management team.

"Seriously," said still another, "remember when you gave me time off without question when my husband became ill? You didn't need to do that — but you did, and I'll always appreciate that."

The coworker sitting next to her added, "Every year, you find a way to pad our holiday paychecks with a little bonus cash, and we know that comes from your pocket. We all realize you are the only guy working with all of us women, and yet you have a very positive, supportive way of helping us work through our conflicts and disagreements without getting frustrated or angry with us."

All the team members were able to share examples of when Nick had stepped into the role of Nurturer/Companion with poise and professionalism.

"This led to an intriguing conversation about why he didn't want to acknowledge his talent for this role," Juli says, "and, consequently, why traditional business cultures — especially in a conservative industry like banking — more often reinforce Dominant and Predator-like behavior. Nick assumed that the Nurturer/Companion role was too 'soft,' when in fact, every time he had employed it, it represented a powerful leadership decision that built a culture of trust and loyalty."

The discussion also revealed that, at times, people did look to Nick to engage the Dominant role, especially related to cross-departmental conflicts, time-sensitive decisions, or situations in which bank policies or procedures were being compromised and the managers were at an impasse regarding what action to take next.

"In these examples, the team wanted and needed the president to step into a more directive, take-charge position so resolution could occur," Juli emphasized. "Nick himself was well aware of incidents that required him to take on the Dominant role, but he admitted that, previous to taking the Master Herder assessment, he would have described himself as *being* dominant 'all the time.' He hadn't considered that employing the Nurturer/Companion role was also a way to lead. Completing the Master Herder assessment inadvertently brought a new perspective on what truly masterful, mature leadership is. And for this retired marine, it was eye opening."

## Additional Benefits of a Mature Human Nurturer/Companion

Appreciates diversity.

Facilitates the integration of new members into any social system.

Strengthens bonds and builds trust through understanding, affection, and connection.

Offers appropriate, timely support to those in need.

Encourages mutual aid over competition.

Creates a patient, nurturing *space* for growth, rather than trying to force or unduly control growth.

Supports *process* in any organization, leading to increased productivity for the entire group.

## A Gift and a Curse

In well-socialized herbivores, most herd members show solid nurturing and companionship skills, even those who are herd Dominants or Leaders. In humans, however, many people either under- or overemphasize nurturing and companionship skills (often by having a single role forced upon them through rigid gender stereotypes). This can become toxic to the group. The dysfunctions exemplified by Nurturer/Companions who lack proficiency in the other roles are usually unintentional, a result of the unconscious power plays these people engage in when they haven't developed other forms of power.

People who excel in this role demonstrate a keen awareness of others' needs and emotions, sometimes to a fault. Gifted Nurturer/Companions become experts at calming others — in part because *they* can't relax until everyone else in the vicinity feels comfortable. When lacking proficiency in the other roles, such people are likely to lose touch with their own feelings and opinions, or fail to be assertive even when they do know what they want, steadily increasing confusion and frustration over time.

The situation intensifies exponentially if they live and work with people who lack proficiency in this role. Because a particularly intuitive Nurturer/Companion offers support before others have to ask for it, he or she assumes that others would quite naturally do the same in return if they truly cared. Colleagues, employees, and family members who overemphasize one of the other roles, however, are unlikely to return the favor — not because they disrespect this person, but because they aren't paying attention to *anyone's* needs at that same level.

Adding further insult to injury, overidentifying with the Nurturer/Companion role practically guarantees a person will be passed over for promotions. Once again, this isn't because coworkers dislike the person or devalue his or her loyalty and support, but because attitudes and behaviors common to this role will compromise the person's ability to lead if these qualities aren't balanced by solid, mature, assertiveness skills.

### Challenges of a Human Nurturer/Companion

Is less likely to lead because of interest in keeping everyone comfortable and together.

Has trouble differentiating between assertiveness and aggression.

Sees the Dominant as abusive, but will try to get close to such a person, inspiring "two-faced" behavior.

Power tends to "go underground" through passive-aggressive
    moves and grudge holding.
Cannot "dial up" power over a "5" without adding frustration or
    rage, leading to embarrassment and sometimes shame.
Tends to use gossip as a bonding tool.

## Toxic Nurturing

Many women entering the workforce in the 1960s, 1970s, and 1980s
operated at a serious disadvantage. Trained to develop the nurturing
arts at the exclusion of the other roles, these intelligent, well-meaning
"good girls" not only had to deal with overt discrimination; some became their own worst enemies when they finally did get promoted.

"Gina," a forty-seven-year-old counselor, described several classic
Nurturer/Companion dilemmas when she contacted me about some
difficulties with her management team. Her small East Coast social service agency was experiencing high turnover due to significant interpersonal unrest at all levels of the organization. "I feel like I'm going
crazy," she said. "Most everyone here has some kind of training or advanced degree in psychology or social work, but we're having trouble
serving our clients because the *staff* can't seem to get along."

During several phone sessions, I gained insight into some unproductive dynamics, including the employment of what I now recognize
as a predictable leadership "coup" engaged by an ambitious Nurturer/
Companion.

In the first place, the entire organization was suffering from an
overabundance of people who lacked assertiveness skills. Experienced
caregivers who were promoted had trouble leading others through
the stressful by-products of organizational change, simply because
their nurturing instincts caused them to constantly check in with people to make sure they were "comfortable." As a result, any forward

movement was ponderous at best, with some planning meetings taking on the pallor of group counseling sessions.

The Nurturer/Companion's fixation on comfort over assertiveness also made it difficult for staff members who overidentified with this role to hold people accountable for unproductive behavior. Far too many employees released the pressure through clandestine conversations that undermined coworkers who were, in some circles, secretly demonized.

Gina conceded that many people were employing the "armchair psychologist" power play. For instance, more dominant coworkers who occasionally attacked others for little or no reason and "refused to move" when asked were diagnosed with "oppositional defiant disorder." The unspoken stress increased when one of these people, "Terrance," was promoted to a significant management position — specifically because he proved capable of motivating resistant employees. With most people abdicating the Dominant role, Terrance increasingly became the bad guy who everyone else depended upon to keep staff in line.

"Evelyn," the founder of the agency, possessed a PhD in psychology. With solid nurturing/companionship skills, she nonetheless found herself increasingly preoccupied with the leadership role. Long-range planning, organizational demands, and meetings with community members understandably prevented her from checking in with staff.

As a result, she depended upon "Molly," her administrative assistant, to take the pulse of the group and report back if conflicts and other interpersonal issues became a serious hindrance to the agency's effectiveness.

On the surface, Molly was soft-spoken, supportive, and knowledgeable, especially when it came to office politics. "She's really smart and perceptive," Gina told me. "But she was passed over for a promotion a couple of years ago, mostly because she's kind of wishy-washy, I guess. Still, she's really good at helping others, and I think that puts her in a kind of informal staff counseling position that she's not actually getting paid for."

As I interviewed Gina further, I could see that Molly possessed the classic strengths *and* challenges of the Nurturer/Companion role. Raised in a conservative Southern family, the fifty-seven-year-old woman had dropped out of college to marry her high school sweetheart. After staying home for twenty years, she entered the workforce in her early forties to help fund her children's education.

"Molly tends to gossip more than she should, but she's also one of the most naturally therapeutic people I know," Gina continued. "Staff members often confide in her. But she never went back to college to finish her degree, so she can't be promoted to working with clients. And as far as managing others is concerned, it's like she has no backbone. She's perpetually stuck in an assistant role, and I can tell that's frustrating for her. But she has a lot of influence behind the scenes."

That "influence" turned out to be the bottleneck of the agency's most significant problems. Through a series of quiet conversations with key employees, Molly was subtly undermining both Terrance and Evelyn, creating a gulf between the administration on one side and the office staff and social workers on the other.

An imbalance of roles in all employees was the root of the dysfunction: The agency's dynamics caused Evelyn to overemphasize the Leader role, making her appear aloof and self-absorbed at times. As the most-assertive, decisive manager, Terrance was pretty much forced to overemphasize the Dominant role. And Molly, who didn't *seem* to have an ambitious bone in her body, unconsciously capitalized on these factors to gain influence with the rest of the staff by perpetually conveying, in so many words and gestures, the idea that, in essence, "Terrance is abusive. Evelyn cares more about the mission than she does about any of us. But *I* care. Come to *me* when you need a shoulder to cry on or support in getting anything done around here."

In the process, Molly had amassed a significant group of followers, becoming the agency's secret leader, one who built loyalty through nurturing behavior that was free of goals or consequences. After all, she depended on Evelyn and Terrance to make the unpopular decisions and lead or push people out of their comfort zones. At the same time, Molly drew attention to the classic challenges resulting from Evelyn overemphasizing the Leader role and Terrance taking on the truly thankless job of company Dominant.

Even so, neither Evelyn nor Terrance noticed this dynamic for a very specific reason: Molly exhibited supportive behavior toward both of them as well. This wasn't a premeditated, calculating, two-faced move; rather, a talented Nurturer/Companion strives to make *everyone* feel welcome and comfortable. Molly's training in the social graces befitting a Southern belle upped the ante on her skills in this arena. As a result, she would empathize with someone who had dealt with the "wrath of Terrance" in the morning, hear Terrance's side of the story in the afternoon, and look for some way to smooth things over between the protagonists by the weekend.

Without the time to write a grant for staff training in the Master Herder model, the agency sent Gina to a workshop at my Arizona ranch. Because other staff members wouldn't have the same information, Gina knew it would be challenging to shift the dysfunctional dynamics when she returned, but she was inspired by the potential.

"That's why you need to hurry up and write a book on this subject so I can share it with the staff," she laughed. "Still, I was able to share the handouts on the five roles at a management meeting, and it opened up some discussion. Evelyn says she's committed to having key staff members do some assertiveness training next year, and Molly will be among those attending. If nothing else, that should relieve some of the pressure Terrance is under. But most important, having a different perspective has given me more patience, clarity, and compassion toward everyone. I don't see staff members as acting crazy anymore. I know that they are simply lacking balance in certain roles."

## A Dangerous Place

At the opposite end of the spectrum, we see dysfunction take hold of people who neglect or actively avoid developing proficiency in nurturing and companionship skills. Remember: The computer software company that hired sociometrist Greg Reid wasn't just concerned about

Melanie's seemingly low productivity; management also wanted insight into the high-performing yet socially inhibited "curmudgeons." Intellectual geniuses who hide in their offices are less likely to hold leadership positions, and they are more likely to experience interpersonal and motivational complications if they are promoted. But that's just the tip of the iceberg. As history shows over and over again, the world becomes a very dangerous place when powerful people abdicate the Nurturer/Companion role. Even worse, leaders who overemphasize the Predator and Dominant roles create social structures that devalue — and in certain contexts practically outlaw — compassionate, collaborative, life-enhancing behavior.

At this point, I could list thousands of sadistic dictators and terrorist organizations from modern times right on back through the dawn of civilization. But I'd like to offer an unconventional view of how and why this happens through a timely case study: Fulani men who, either by force or choice, give up their herds for an urban lifestyle.

Though the Fulani's origins are sketchy, these tribes "apparently began their penetration of the study area in northern Nigeria between AD 1350 and 1450," Dale Lott and Benjamin Hart wrote in the 1979 article I cited earlier. "At the time of the European colonization of the area they had achieved political domination of virtually all the local populations, although they were outnumbered at least four to one." History therefore suggests that the ability of a single herder to hold his own with an angry Fulani bull one minute, herd several dozen cattle away from tempting crops the next, and lead them all happily back to camp at the end of the day has significant repercussions for leading and/or dominating large groups of people as well.

But remember, like all pastoralists, the Fulani traditionally spend much more time engaging in nurturing and sentinel activities than in dominant, leadership, or predator-based behavior. Caring for animals releases oxytocin, buffering fight-or-flight instincts in favor of a calm-and-connect response.

When these people are separated from their cattle, however, the hormone no longer modulates the aggressive energy that young herders eventually transform into mature assertiveness. City-based Fulani women continue to experience an oxytocin release in childbirth, milk production, and caring for their families. But adolescent males in particular lack the biochemical support to soften and socialize their immense power once they no longer have daily contact with their animals.

"The Fulani's formula of intimacy and aggression, courage and understanding, sounds like a description of how oxytocin and vasopressin promote social interactions," Meg Daley Olmert contends in *Made for Each Other.* "We know that oxytocin can flow between humans and animals, and it's possible that vasopressin does as well." However, when the calm-and-connect response of oxytocin is dramatically reduced, if not removed, from an adolescent Fulani male's system due to loss of the herding lifestyle, the vasopressin surge of aggression can still be exercised through gang-like behavior among young men living in cities. In this way, the once-balanced power this genetic line developed over centuries lacks the moderation that caring for cattle once provided.

For this reason, I was saddened and concerned (though not surprised) to find that the Fulani culture Lott and Hart chronicled forty years earlier was approaching extinction. Like the Apaches who once roamed freely through southern Arizona, across the very lands where my horses and I recovered a hint of this ancient wisdom, Africa's nomadic tribes were systematically being assimilated into a sedentary life that offered them poverty, disconnection, confusion, and depression (an emotion the Fulani didn't have a word for in the 1970s).

Like the Apache in the late-nineteenth century, twenty-first-century Fulani have their own Geronimos who violently rebel at times. And they seem destined to suffer a similar fate. But the situation is far more dangerous in Africa. Muslim extremists are recruiting impressionable Fulani youth to take out their anger and frustration on "the enemies of Allah." No longer encouraged to balance the five roles, these immature, disenfranchised herders are trained to suppress the Nurturer/Companion role, while identifying exclusively with a Predator-Dominant combination. As a result, these intensely powerful young men exhibit a truly astonishing aptitude for terrorism.

# CHAPTER SIX

# Observe and Alert:
# The Sentinel's Perspective

*Role: Sentinel*

There's much to envy about the horse — speed, strength, agility, grace, beauty, and something else, something that even people driving the latest 420-horsepower SUV will never approximate through technology: the ability to sleep standing up.

A special feature of equine anatomy, known as the "stay apparatus," allows the muscles to rest while certain joints, bones, and ligaments lock the legs in place. In this position, horses can engage the body's revitalizing "slow-wave sleep," in which electrical activity in the brain lengthens and decelerates, quieting and renewing the mind. It helps to have four limbs for optimal balance, of course, but imagine the benefits in human situations: giving in to the Thanksgiving turkey stupor while you stand in some static department store line waiting for the doors to open on Black Friday. Catching some much-needed rest outside your local stadium a few hours before tickets to a coveted concert or sports event go on sale.

Still, even horses must lie down to dream. Brain waves become short and fast during REM (rapid eye movement) sleep, indicating the same kinds of informational processing that humans experience in a similar state. The body must be fully relaxed to enter this stage of sleep, though horses will sometimes neigh and move their legs as if running.

Some of these dreams no doubt involve racing full-throttle across a high desert plain. Others seem more frantic and disturbing: muffled whinnies alerting the herd to primal threats, nightmarish escapes from larger-than-life lions, fantasies involving mating escapades or fights with rival stallions.

No matter how ecstatic or terrifying the vision, however, horses must feel reasonably safe in the "real" world to lie down and surrender to REM. Otherwise, they'll choose to doze standing up, day after day. In the most extreme cases, they take on the nervous demeanor of sleep-deprived humans, eventually collapsing during slow-wave sleep due to long-term mind and muscle fatigue.

Here's where the Sentinel serves as guardian of the herd's well-being. That one horse you see standing over the others as they dream is the perfect example. Only it's not just one horse, of course. All mature herd members trade this role on and off throughout the day so that everyone can rest, eat, play, mate, give birth, and in general, enjoy life, even as carnivores wander in and out of view.

### Characteristics of a Human or Animal Sentinel

Scans environment so that others can securely interact, relax, dream, or do their job.

Steps away from the herd to witness threats and opportunities from a wider perspective.

Sometimes actively protects the herd (when also possessing Dominant skills).

Sometimes alerts the group to predators, inclement weather, and other dangers on the horizon.

### Someone to Watch Over Me

When Brandi, Leyla, and Savannah first came to my ranch, these understandably vigilant mares rotated sentinel shifts religiously. But after a few weeks, all three began to lie down together, a sure sign they were relaxing into our safe, congenial, horse-friendly environment. Upon waking, however, they still endeavored to keep one another in sight at all times. Leading one member of this tight little band away for training would initially send the other two into a panic. So for the first year, any horse-facilitated learning activities involving the Spice Girls took place in a round pen set up inside their large corral. Under these conditions, the mares proved to be quick learners, and they were exceptional teachers of our human students. As long as we respected that Leyla, Brandi, and Savannah drew strength and confidence from watching — and watching out for — one another, their curiosity in the world around them and their interest in meeting new people grew daily.

Over time, through increasing trust in their human caretakers, the Spice Girls learned to tolerate progressively longer periods of separation. But I'll never forget the first day I brought Leyla out to work with some advanced students on the other side of the property. Initially, "Karen" was a bit concerned when the blue-eyed mare trotted around the arena, calling out to Brandi and Savannah, who were whinnying in the distance. As expected, Leyla calmed down once the woman used various leadership techniques to focus the mare's attention and gain her cooperation. After about ten minutes of movement-oriented activities, Karen appropriately paused to praise the horse while gently rubbing her neck and withers.

Then, with the best of intentions, my student did something that unnerved Leyla. Karen, a gifted Nurturer/Companion who was still a bit uncomfortable with the Leader and Dominant roles, knelt down to, as she put it, "make myself smaller, to show that I was not so intimidating, that I respected Leyla and was willing to trust her." Whereupon the mare backed up in surprise and trotted to the opposite end of the corral, calling out to Brandi and Savannah as she paced back and forth. Leyla's movements weren't frantic; she clearly wasn't afraid of Karen. Rather, it seemed more like the horse was actively requesting assistance.

Karen and I were both perplexed. I had seen several people take this vulnerable position with Leyla in the past, usually with tears in their eyes as the mare gently touched the tops of their heads with her soft muzzle, standing over them with a warm, peaceful, motherly demeanor. Then it suddenly dawned on me. Leyla had always been with *her* herd in *their* corral during those sessions. This time, she was in new territory without the benefit of Brandi or Savannah watching, listening, witnessing, protecting.

"Wait a minute," I said, walking over to Karen. "I think I know what's going on. When you knelt down, you unknowingly asked Leyla to act as Sentinel for you in an unfamiliar situation. But she was just gaining confidence in this environment through *your* support. Without the herd backing her up, she wasn't capable of looking out for you at that moment."

To test this theory, I caught Leyla's attention and walked unconcerned halfway around the outside of the arena to show that I felt perfectly safe and content in this area. Then I planted myself ten feet away from the fence in a stance that conveyed I was simultaneously scanning the environment and gently observing Leyla and Karen. The blue-eyed mare sighed with relief, walked over to the woman, and engaged in a tender mutual grooming session, fully relaxed, confident that a trusted two-legged herd member was watching over them both.

## Neighborhood Watch

When employing the Sentinel role, working Master Herders aren't merely scanning the landscape for lions and wolves. These people are also noticing herd dynamics in relation to environmental influences, paying attention to opportunities as well as threats on the horizon. Modern city dwellers, on the other hand, rely on law enforcement professionals to combine the protective functions of a Dominant with the surveillance capabilities of a Sentinel. In this sense, the predator-detection function of the latter role is separated out from its traditionally much wider orientation of supporting community well-being.

In the 1960s, however, an increasing burglary rate in rural and suburban areas resulted in a citizen-based crime prevention program that eventually resurrected some of the Sentinel's life-enhancing benefits as well. Based on multiple requests from sheriffs and police chiefs around the country, the National Neighborhood Watch Program was officially established in 1972. The roots of this program can actually be traced back to the days of colonial settlements, when night watchmen patrolled the streets. In the late-twentieth century, as two-income families became the norm, many neighborhoods were deserted during the day. Criminals capitalized on this factor, taxing law enforcement to its limits. Communities that received training and encouragement in observing and reporting suspicious behavior experienced lower crime rates. These impressive statistics eventually warranted a grant to take the neighborhood watch concept national.

As the movement evolved, it expanded from an "extra eyes and ears" approach to a much more proactive, community-oriented endeavor that not only addressed crime prevention issues but also restored neighborhood pride and unity. The organization's website reports that it's "not uncommon to see members of Neighborhood Watch groups participating in community cleanups and other activities that strive to improve the quality of life for community residents." Meetings also offer "a useful forum for airing neighborhood problems and practicing problem-solving techniques."

In the process, neighborhood watch groups have helped people around the country more fully reclaim the Sentinel's age-old function. The nature of the organization encourages civilians to trade the role so that every responsible adult develops this caring, observational awareness — while keeping those who might otherwise be obliged to overemphasize this role from burning out.

### Additional Benefits of a Human Sentinel

Observes social dynamics within the group as well as how the group interacts with the environment, culture, or larger economy or society.

Engages a relaxed yet heightened awareness of the big picture in the moment (Leaders focus on the big picture in the future).

Alerts Leaders when the community or organization is losing track of its purpose or is in need of support and protection.

Serves as a holder of group consciousness who stays on the edges but remains tuned in to the group's life and work, ideally keeping its welfare in mind and heart.

"Smells smoke before others see the fire."

Acts as a "whistleblower" when necessary.

Fosters calmness and trust so others can rest, play, interact, or do their work without vigilance.

## The Power of the Witness

From Pennsylvania to Florida, Texas, Colorado, and California, small towns and big cities across the United States publish newspapers called *The Sentinel*. The popularity of this title speaks to a widespread understanding of the importance of this role, which for a time became a highly specialized profession requiring equal parts observation, investigation, and writing ability.

In the twentieth century, journalists further capitalized on the latest technology as radio, television, cable news networks, and satellite capabilities brought events from the farthest reaches of the planet into our living rooms instantaneously. Today, with the advent of social media and cell phone cameras, large numbers of people with no journalistic training or media connections have taken on the Sentinel role with gusto. And the world has suddenly become a much more level playing field.

Political and business leaders might still be able to buy or control the press, but when your average citizen can video atrocities, acts of heroism, and everything in between — uploading these images to the internet with a few key strokes on a hand-held device — dictators and other human predators are much more likely to be held accountable for behavior that was easy to hide two decades ago.

As we reclaim the power to observe and alert people to threats and opportunities, however, it's important to highlight a vital element of the Sentinel's traditional role: compassion and concern for the "herd's" well-being. Otherwise, the role devolves into disconnected, cynical, and in some cases, intensely predatory behavior. A carnivorous Sentinel essentially becomes a lone wolf, crouching in the grass, looking to capture evidence of others' mistakes, vulnerabilities, and interpersonal faux pas — *not* to help the community *course correct*, but to gain some personal advantage, be it money, status, a lucrative promotion, or revenge.

Juli Lynch deals with predatory Sentinels in the banking industry; these are upper level managers who shrewdly observe market shifts in relation to the organization's strengths and weaknesses. Only these professionals aren't sharing the information with colleagues; they're waiting for the right moment to capitalize on trends that others ignore: to oust the CEO, profit from a hostile takeover, or gain a better position with another company willing to pay for insights into the competition.

It's important to remember, however, that most people who over-emphasize the Sentinel role do so with the best of intentions. Still, the tendency to step back and look at the big picture may be devalued or, at the very least, misunderstood:

Responding to rumors of another economic crisis, a father who deeply cares about his family's welfare may come across as aloof and unresponsive to his children's dreams and emotional needs as he faithfully manages the household budget, cutting music lessons and other "superfluous" expenses.

The wife and business partner of a local furniture dealer might see unproductive staff dynamics and their effect on the bottom line precisely because she's not working at the store daily — and is thus less susceptible to office politics and interpersonal dramas. Yet when she shares her concerns, she may be dismissed as a meddling spouse.

Much more infuriating is the keenly observant, intensely intelligent

Sentinel who brings problems to the table without ever lifting a finger to offer viable solutions, moderate conflict, or correct unproductive behavior. These people instead appeal to the nearest Leader or Dominant to take action rather than developing proficiency in those roles themselves.

## Challenges of a Human Sentinel

Can be seen as overly logical, aloof, and detached.

Tends to emphasize group needs at the expense of individual needs and desires.

Sometimes suffers from Leaders and Dominants who prefer to "shoot the messenger" rather than heed the Sentinel's warnings or advice.

May be tempted to use information for personal gain rather than for the group's welfare (by failing to alert others to impending disaster or opportunities).

May focus on spreadsheets, budgets, data, and procedures rather than emotions, interpersonal dynamics, and the creativity of others.

Can become hypervigilant and problem-focused without offering solutions or helping to intervene in conflict or create new policies or products.

## The Lookout

Ideally, responsible adults perform the Sentinel function, with adolescents learning the art gently over time. However, in families with parental drug abuse, depression, and mental illness, youngsters will often take on the role, sometimes instinctually, sometimes under the tutelage of older siblings and friends.

"A popular practice among homeless youth, children in foster care,

and those who have come in contact with the juvenile justice system is 'keeping watch,' an informal code of the street," says Susan
Crimmins, LCSW, PhD, an Eponaquest faculty member and equine-
facilitated learning specialist who worked for many years as a forensic
social worker and a criminologist. "This role of Sentinel typically is
assumed by a younger person, as a way to earn their keep and to prove
loyalty to 'family.' I have known children as young as eight to assume
this role in exchange for food and makeshift shelter with the hope that
they finally can belong to a tribe where they will be kept safe."

As Susan told me in an email interview:

In juvenile justice literature, the idea of a "lookout" was well
documented as instrumental in gang and group behaviors for
the very purpose of ensuring protection and safety among de-
linquent youth. In addition, youth who live on the streets or
who are in "temporary" foster care often adopt a Sentinel role
as a way to demonstrate their value to others, sometimes in an
effort to seek stability in addition to their seeking safety.

In my career as a forensic social worker, I recall one particular young man, Jesse (a pseudonym), who was serving time
on probation for robbery. He said he had learned his lesson
and would not commit any more crimes because he had found
a way to earn money, which was to make himself invaluable
to others by keeping watch for people in his neighborhood.
When I inquired as to what this looked like, Jesse explained
that he would be on the lookout for welfare workers' arrivals,
potential thefts of local businesses, threats to local gang members, all for a trade of solid food, clean clothes, and a small fee
from local businesses and gang members. In his foster family,
he had learned quickly to avoid the wrath of his foster parents by alerting them to landlord and social services visits and
diverting them whenever possible. Fiercely protective of the
adults in his world, Jesse quickly learned that his watchkeeper
role would afford him a valuable place of being needed, and

therefore, making himself indispensable. He was only eleven years old when he began serving as Sentinel at home and in his community.

While many of her clients were too young to gain more formal employment themselves, Susan also saw instances of youngsters actively seeking jobs for parents. By making connections with community members, some of these children exhibited an unusually mature, socially intelligent use of the Sentinel as a leadership role, in this case modeling the much more enlightened skill of scanning the environment for opportunities, with the goal of promoting an increased sense of well-being for the tribe as a whole.

## Mindfulness in Action

The Sentinel seems to emerge instinctually in certain individuals when groups lack food, shelter, and the protection of strong, caring adults. Once our basic needs are met, this witnessing form of consciousness takes on sophisticated mental health and creativity-enhancing features.

It's no surprise that people naturally talented in this role are often attracted to studying mindfulness and meditation. Here the Sentinel perspective is employed to dispassionately watch one's own mind, emotions, and responses to the environment. While this practice was developed in Asia — initially associated with Buddhist and Taoist traditions — the Western world began to develop secularized forms of mindfulness training in the late-twentieth century.

Jon Kabat-Zinn's Mindfulness-Based Stress Reduction (MBSR) program, created at the University of Massachusetts Medical School in 1979, launched a host of clinical studies that documented the physical and mental health benefits of mindfulness in general and of MBSR in particular. Similar models have been widely adopted in schools, prisons, hospitals, counseling centers, veterans' programs, and other environments.

Many companies have incorporated the practice into their culture. Apple, Procter & Gamble, General Mills, Raytheon, New Balance,

Bose, and Monsanto are among those corporations offering mindfulness coaching, resulting in better employee well-being, lower levels of frustration, and an improved overall work environment. Additionally, employees who've embraced these programs exhibit lower levels of absenteeism and burnout.

A number of books extol the benefits of mindfulness training in business settings, including Michael Carroll's *Awake at Work* (2004) and *The Mindful Leader* (2007), as well as the bestseller *Resonant Leadership: Renewing Yourself and Connecting with Others through Mindfulness, Hope, and Compassion* (2005) by Richard E. Boyatzis and Annie McKee.

Critics of secularized methods, however, argue that they encourage some people to become more aloof and detached — which are, curiously enough, symptoms associated with anyone who overemphasizes the Sentinel role. Steve Jobs is the by-now-classic example of a leader who used his interest in Zen meditation to justify emotionally disconnected behavior. While the mind-training benefits are especially clear in Job's case, the original Buddhist practice emphasized compassionate engagement with all sentient beings, a feature often lost in modern Westernized programs. In taking on the Sentinel role, horses model a caring, socially engaged form of mindfulness that has much more in common with the original Eastern orientation.

Mary-Louise Gould, EdM, an Eponaquest instructor and faculty member, specializes in teaching mindfulness practices through working with horses. It's no coincidence that she was the person who recommended I add the Sentinel to the Master Herder model as an important aspect of balanced, socially intelligent leadership. Unlike Jobs and other high-powered executives who've studied mindfulness, Mary-Louise, an educator and therapist, puts the heart front and center in her trainings — as did the original founder of this age-old practice, Siddhartha Gautama. Known more famously as the Buddha, he was also, interestingly enough, an exceptional horseman. In chapter 10 of *The Power of the Herd*, I argue that he gained rudimentary mindfulness skills from working with these animals, which sparked his interest in honing the sophisticated techniques he later devised for people.

As I have always emphasized, horses embody many of the attitudes people access through more formal meditation practices, including the ability to engage fully with reality. What seems so difficult for a grasping, hoarding, controlling, and competitive human being comes easily to these intensely aware, nomadic, nonpredatory power animals. Horses are actually hardwired for the state of nonattachment championed by the Buddha. In the wild, they don't defend territory, build nests, live in caves, or store nuts for the winter. They move unprotected with the rhythms of nature, cavorting through the snow, kicking up their heels on cool spring mornings, grazing peacefully in fields of flowing grass, despite a keen and constant awareness of predators lurking in the distance. While they react quickly in the face of danger, they also show remarkable resilience in recovering from traumatic events. They don't ruminate over and over and over again about the injustices of the past, clouding their vision and their enjoyment of life with ceaseless internal dialogues about how cruel it is that God invented lions.

The simple truth of the matter is that when you act more horselike — when you stop ruminating on the past and planning for the future, when you let go of preconceived notions and simply notice what *is* happening from moment to moment, as opposed to judging what *should* or *shouldn't* happen — you are practicing mindfulness. It's easier said than done, of course, because the human ego relentlessly strives to defend its self-serving theories. People who are invested in their own superiority, for instance, will record and replay experiences that bolster this view while ignoring evidence suggesting that other people, races, or species also have valid perspectives and gifts. Fanatics will go so far as to start wars and even martyr themselves to uphold a limited or fraudulent belief system.

The alternative true mindfulness offers is the ability to see the world as it is while imagining fresh ways of relating to an ever-emerging, more richly nuanced vision of reality. You will, at times, remember the past (as opposed to obsessing on it) and plan for the future (without becoming overly attached to one particular scheme). With your mental faculties revealing the truth, as opposed to defending a self-image, you'll begin to live life as an improvisatory *art* as opposed to a rigid formula. In the process, you'll gain access to untapped resources of emotional resilience, clarity, enthusiasm, satisfaction, and creativity.

People who cultivate a serious mindfulness practice often describe innovative ideas emerging seemingly from out of nowhere. It is as if this patient, nonjudgmental, yet discerning witnessing function clears away the clutter, allowing the psyche to relax, to take in new information, and finally, to dream. The challenge lies in manifesting these visions.

Those who overindulge their inner Sentinel, however, are rarely successful in entrepreneurial endeavors and long-term creative projects. The keen observer must give way to an inner Leader that can champion the vision and rally others to the cause, an inner Dominant that can push forward when difficulties arise and enthusiasm wanes, an inner Predator that can pick two or three worthy goals and respectfully cull the rest, and an inner Nurturer/Companion that supports daily health and well-being. Otherwise, you may find yourself among the many frustrated artists sitting around in coffeehouses packed with other would-be musicians, novelists, and inventors, who amuse one another with compelling insights, glib repartee, profound but undeveloped journal entries, and exciting concepts that never truly see the light of day.

# CHAPTER SEVEN

# Cull and Recalibrate:
# The Predator's Sacred Task

## *Role: Predator*

O f all the Master Herder roles, the Predator is the most dangerous. Thoughtlessly overemphasizing or intentionally misusing this power results in destructive behavior that can wreak havoc for generations, setting cycles of trauma and revenge in motion that compromise the mental, emotional, and social evolution of entire cultures. Whether they're engaged in business, politics, family, or community endeavors, people who overidentify with this role can keep otherwise intelligent and creative populations in a state of arrested development through the demoralizing effects of cruelty and fear. It goes without saying that all terrorist organizations fully align with, if not worship, this carnivorous brand of power.

Even so, nature shows us that *proper* use of the Predator is essential, not only for keeping life in balance with available resources, but also for fostering growth and transformation through death and recalibration. This enigma has fascinated philosophers since the beginning of recorded history. But it becomes an integrated, multifaceted reality when you live with large animals and call them by name.

In nomadic animal-centered cultures, people exercise compassion, connection, and thoughtfulness to keep their inner Predator in check. Rather than callously thriving at others' expense, as dictators and predatory business factions are inclined to do, the relationship between two-legged and four-legged tribe members is consciously symbiotic. To nourish his family, a man may slaughter a cow he steadfastly nurtured through birth, childhood, and lameness or sickness. The next day this same herder may lose his own life protecting the herd.

Humans aren't alone in negotiating the pastoralist's paradox. Herding dogs must also modify their carnivorous instincts to harmonize with herbivores that have very different responses to threats and challenges. Sometimes these domesticated wolves are injured or even killed protecting animals their ancestors considered prey; other times, they show remarkable self-control in standing up to aggressive bulls and stallions — without hurting, or getting hurt, in the process.

Sedentary people who treat animals as sentient beings (rather than as mechanistic commodities) develop similar abilities, especially when they thoughtfully socialize their four-legged companions, rather than rely exclusively on dominance, restraint, and confinement. Working with a combination of predatory and nonpredatory species heightens the fluid perspective that allows modern humans to balance all five of the Master Herder roles.

## Rites of Passage

Since that pivotal moment when my mare Rasa protected my dog, Nala, and me from a herd of free-range cattle, I've had many opportunities to study the differences between carnivore and herbivore behavior, learning, in the process, to balance the strengths of both — in the external life of our multispecies culture and in the ecosystem of my own psyche. I've also performed the Predator's most sacred task with over a dozen canine and equine companions. Euthanizing valued herd members as a result of old age or debilitating illness is a heart-wrenching decision in itself. Taking the time to honor them, say good-bye, and hold them during those final, most precious breaths requires an additional level of emotional heroism.

In the face of inescapable loss, people may understandably ask a spouse to take the family pet to the clinic, walk away from a beloved horse when the vet arrives, or perhaps intellectualize the experience and thereby disconnect from the pain of it. Over the years, I've gained increasing capacity to witness and support both humans and animals in their final moments by calling upon my "inner lion." This becomes even more essential when I'm the one who must make the decision to euthanize a four-legged family member. To willingly join the team of professionals pledged to end suffering by literally ending a life, I must draw strength from the predatory side of my own omnivorous soul. While I may cry or even scream out the horror of it in private hours after the burial, my heart expands each time I open my arms wide to the gift, responsibility, and mystery of caring for another being, knowing all along that I'm likely to outlive individuals who have touched me so deeply that my world will change irrevocably when they're gone.

In the process, I've gained increasing facility in using the Predator role for other purposes. Respectfully and compassionately culling a habit, belief, business practice, or relationship that has reached the limits of its productivity also diminishes suffering, brings balance to any system, and opens up space and resources for new growth.

### Benefits of a Mature Human or Animal Predator

Keeps life in balance with available resources.
Culls what is no longer needed.
Exhibits keen sensitivity to energy and resource drains.
Makes tough decisions during lean times.
Ends suffering through euthanasia.
Offers additional protection from predators.

## Torrid Tails

Seven years ago, I adopted two puppies, sisters from the same litter. Their border-collie mother passed down a herding gene that her children embraced with gusto. Flint and Mica eventually learned to control this impulse — but only at my insistence. Even today, they still believe that all horses are just begging to be chased.

No one knew who the father was, but as these feisty little dogs matured, I began to suspect their sire was a pit bull or some other sturdy, aggressive, dog-fighting breed. His lineage produced another, completely unexpected challenge in socializing Flint and Mica: teaching them to live with *each other*.

For the better part of a year, the lively, adorable, black-and-white-spotted sisters were inseparable, exploring the world, playing, and sleeping together. Then, without warning, something changed. "Sibling rivalry" was too mild a term for the savage, territorial fights that broke out, battles so fierce that I had to put their beds and feeding bowls in separate rooms. To this day, I must instruct Flint to wait at the bottom of the stairs until I close the door to Mica's room at the top, or the two will wage a terrifying war in the second-story hallway. I've since heard from several dog trainers that canine sisters are known for this kind of behavior, and that if I valued a peaceful household, I should have chosen between the two or picked a male-female combination with dogs from the same litter. Ah, the wisdom of hindsight...

Hair-raising incidents aside, Flint and Mica have afforded me an ongoing education in predatory group dynamics, revealing nuances I never would have grasped if I'd been smart enough to adopt only one of them. In the first place, they exhibit the classic carnivore characteristic of valuing territory over relationship. If I hadn't been present to break up their most brutal, fur-flying, blood-spattering row, Flint might have literally received the death penalty for entering Mica's room. The ongoing problem from Flint's perspective, however, involves a stash of bones and toys her sister habitually amasses, half of which are stolen. Mica is a cute but sneaky little hoarder who lies in wait for Flint to walk away from a new ball or rawhide twisty treat, whereupon it suddenly disappears into the canine twilight zone behind Mica's bed, which she guards like Fort Knox.

Outside the house, however, the two are best friends. When I announce that it's time to play, Mica will run upstairs, choose one of "her" toys, and actually hand it over to Flint as I open the front door. The girls respectfully trade positions as I throw the ball, each one politely watching the other catch it, return it, and then step back as the other moves forward to take a turn.

Here's the truly interesting part from a predatory power standpoint: In the neutral territory of the great outdoors, Flint and Mica get along famously — until one of them steps on a thorn (which happens almost daily in the desert). At that moment, the *wounded* sister becomes the most vicious dog you'll ever meet. Flint in particular utters growls so resonant and horrifying you'd swear she was channeling a pack of wolves as she limps over to me, glaring at Mica with a look of demonic possession, even as she politely waits for me to remove the painful spike. Five seconds later, both tails are wagging as the sisters resume their good-natured play.

The tendency to become combative when feeling vulnerable is a predictable by-product of living in any predatory system. Because she's instinctually inclined to seek out weak, sick, and injured animals as targets, Flint knows, deep in her bones, that when hurt, even carnivores are likely to become prey. And she doesn't trust her own sister in these moments, probably because she also knows the "fight to the death" impulse runs strong in them both. Nonpredatory animals like horses, on the other hand, stop fighting when an aggressor backs off. They also tend to protect, rather than attack, vulnerable herd members.

Predatory logic tells Flint that, when she's injured, it's better to suddenly appear intensely aggressive to *discourage* a physical altercation than to take the very real chance she might have to defend herself in a compromised state. If violence ensues because of Mica's own instinct to attack any animal showing weakness, the smell of blood might send them both into an uncontrollable frenzy.

Humans who've grown up in predatory environments exhibit similar behavior. The impulse to become aggressive when feeling vulnerable, however, is different from an immature Dominant's habit of attacking others for little or no reason. The latter is a predictable, though unproductive, power play. The former is a defensive move. Both sudden shifts in demeanor, however, seem downright crazy to everyone else in the room. Still, it's important to realize that if an otherwise mild-mannered colleague suddenly becomes combative, it's likely that he or she feels vulnerable *and has experienced painful instances of having weaknesses, mistakes, or skill deficiencies used against him or her in the past*. Remember, in conquest-oriented cultures, people are often encouraged, sometimes even taught, to use others' vulnerabilities against them for personal gain.

Regardless of the somewhat understandable reason behind outlandishly defensive behavior, the situation often deteriorates quickly. The aggressor is unlikely to apologize for exploding, let alone share why he or she felt vulnerable. Admitting weakness is dangerous in a predatory power system. Even if the setting is *not* predatory, a person raised by abusive parents in particular will continue to exhibit this knee-jerk reaction long after it has outlived its usefulness. Even worse, he or she will sometimes demand that coworkers apologize profusely for much milder situations where no offense was intended, as if he or she is holding others accountable for previous injustices reactivated by current events. Such a person will feel *justified* in lashing out, even as colleagues perceive that he or she attacked *them*.

If, like Flint and Mica, humans could go back to playing or working together after the thorn is removed, the damage would be minimal. But that rarely occurs, especially in professional situations. In the wake of such an altercation, both sides are subsequently inclined to avoid contact with each other, to talk about the "offenders" behind their backs, to hold a grudge, or sometimes even to seek revenge.

When intentional, highly competitive, "dog-eat-dog" predatory behavior is combined with immature, Dominant power plays, vulnerability-based defensive moves, and the resulting grudges and factions that are created, it's a wonder that groups of people manage to get *anything* done. During a recent workshop, a woman who teaches high school Spanish shared examples of all of these dysfunctional behaviors, explaining how they wreak havoc among students and faculty alike, even though everyone is "supposed" to work together and treat others with respect.

"As I get older, I become more reclusive," she finally said with a heavy sigh. "The people I encounter at school, at church, and even in my own extended family, are so mean at times, so unlikely to admit their mistakes, let alone apologize for the hurtful things they do and say. I'm tired of all the conflict, especially since it seems so profoundly unnecessary. If I win the lottery, I'm going to move to a tropical island and hide out with my husband, my kids, maybe invite a few trusted friends to join us now and then, but for the most part, I'll be sitting out with a book, listening to the waves. I've come to the conclusion that I really don't like *people*, so why should I be around them? I mean, what's the alternative, really?"

"I'm working on it," I said, only half joking. "Over the last ten years, I've learned a few things that actually help. It's a big project though, a multigenerational project. So go ahead and buy that island if the opportunity arises. But don't give up on the human race just yet."

## Challenges of a Human Predator

Exhibits intensely territorial behavior.

Actively scans for shortcomings, mistakes, weaknesses, and skill deficiencies in others and uses these vulnerabilities against them.

Becomes aggressive when he or she feels vulnerable.

Can be too quick to cull sensitive, troubled, less-competitive "herd members," or people who simply need more support and training to excel.

> Sometimes "eats his or her own children," preying on team members, creating rampant mistrust, paranoia, and political games that waste time and money for everyone.
>
> Wants to win at all costs, even when it's not in anyone's best interest.
>
> Overemphasizes a survival-of-the-fittest mentality, transferring competition with other companies to needless and wasteful competition within the company.

## The Dangers of Predatory Intent

Master Herders know that Leader, Dominant, Nurturer/Companion, and Sentinel roles are most effective when they are *consciously separated* from predatory impulses. Predatory power is used thoughtfully and sparingly, mostly to keep the herd and tribe in balance with available resources.

However, in modern sedentary cultures such as our own, predatory behavior is actively promoted in certain circles, causing many people in power to employ dominance, leadership, sentinel, and even nurturing/companionship skills *with an underlying predatory motivation* that can be extremely destructive to the social system as a whole, not to mention confusing and hurtful to individuals.

Pairing predatory power with the role of Dominant, for instance, causes those in leadership positions to become wasteful and abusive. Predatory Dominants feel justified in *thriving* at others' expense, hijacking the resources of the company and the community for short-sighted personal gain. (Dictators revel in this combination.)

Pairing predatory power with the role of Leader results in charismatic individuals who initially build an inspirational presence based on some good ideas of their own, yet who over time feel justified in co-opting others' ideas. Apple's Steve Jobs and Microsoft's Bill Gates have both exhibited this tendency on more than one occasion, sometimes combining it with intensely Dominant behavior.

Pairing predatory power with the role of Sentinel results in the tendency to collect and hoard information on an organization's vulnerabilities to emerging market trends and to cultural or political shifts. Predatory Sentinels use these insights against leaders and colleagues at just the right time to gain personal advantage. For instance, they might facilitate a hostile takeover or sale of a business that results in layoffs for others and in power or profit for themselves. In some industries, this is considered standard practice.

Similarly destructive are Nurturer/Companions who develop predatory tendencies, as they can easily gain an individual's trust, learn about this person's vulnerabilities through intimate conversations, and then suddenly, seemingly inexplicably, use those vulnerabilities against the person for personal gain. Some sociopaths are gifted in this capacity. A sexual predator might single out receptive children by offering them companionship, understanding, and support. Other crafty criminals form alliances with lonely, sick, and/or elderly people by taking care of them and waiting for the right moment to drain the victims' bank accounts.

A Master Herder, on the other hand, employs predatory power with tremendous skill and empathy, for the good of the tribe, the herd, and the ecosystem. In this sense, you might say that he or she uses the role of Predator with *nonpredatory intent*.

## Growing Up in an Intensely Predatory Family System

In taking the Master Herder Professional Assessment, a small percentage of people will exhibit high Predator scores not because they're innately ruthless — or perhaps overfunctioning in this capacity because others refuse to take on the immense responsibility of this role — but because they grew up in an abusive family and are *perpetually on guard*. These sometimes-brilliant employees have hair-trigger responses to minor disagreements. They often state that they feel unsafe in groups.

Most find it difficult to work with peers, and they feel attacked when receiving corrective feedback on their performance. As a result, they show some (not all) of the behaviors associated with overemphasizing the Predator, particularly the tendency to become aggressive when feeling vulnerable and the inclination to cull relationships too quickly. Many also cull themselves from professional, social, or educational situations that others find only mildly stressful. As a result, some of these individuals move from job to job, becoming increasingly frustrated and distrustful of people over time.

You don't have to be a trauma survivor to face significant hurdles in handling conflict productively. Many people avoid confrontation. Other more defiant or spirited individuals attack in response to feeling attacked. Because a previously abused person's motivation is protective (which in the past was for good reason), someone who chooses the latter response tends to be blind to his or her own aggressive behavior. For this reason, it can be very confusing, disturbing, or even demoralizing for such a person to score high on the Predator scale. It is therefore *essential* for these individuals to recognize that they're overrelying on the *vulnerability-based defensive moves* associated with this role as a result of growing up among people who employed additional predatory skills to take advantage of others.

Unlike a cutthroat, alpha-style leader who tries to destroy the competition, people who exhibit this pattern see themselves as victims. Some expect their supervisors to protect them from any colleague who they perceive to be a threat, as if they're seeking resolution at work for a parent who was unwilling or unable to rescue them from childhood physical or sexual assault. This is a particularly difficult pattern for any manager to negotiate, but it's not an uncommon dilemma and sometimes cannot be avoided. (You may find yourself promoted to a department where such an individual works.)

It's important to exhibit compassion for employees and colleagues exhibiting hypervigilant, hyperdefensive tendencies, while encouraging or even requiring them to get additional training and support to alter unproductive behavior. In some situations, companies may also need to hire a coach or consultant to help a supervisor handle this particular challenge.

## Lion-Taming Tips

To truly be effective, the Predator role must be used judiciously, usually with extensive reflection on when and how to employ it. If you're experiencing strong negative emotions, it's better to wait and consider all your options before unleashing your inner carnivore. Fear, frustration, and/or anger may arise when it's time to cull an unproductive relationship, employee, department, or business practice, but these feelings spotlight the *dysfunction*, not the solution. Thoughtful consideration determines the best course of action. (I discuss how to use emotions as information in professional situations in *The Power of the Herd*.)

Adding to the difficulty, employees, constituents, students, and other groups in conflict or competition often want an authority figure to support one faction by *culling* members of another faction. Sometimes, this may be necessary, but it requires a lion's share of self-control to research all the options before making such a decision, particularly when both sides are pressuring you to act in their favor.

For these and other reasons, predatory functions benefit from a visionary leadership perspective, balanced by a mature Nurturer/Companion's compassionate engagement and a nonpredatory Sentinel's view of group dynamics in relation to current business, social, political, and environmental factors.

Recently, for instance, I went through a yearlong period of reorganization inspired by new opportunities and changing market trends.

At the time, I was expanding my horse-facilitated learning center in Arizona, while receiving invitations to lead clinics on five continents, write this book, and consider projects with other leading professionals in my field. After much reflection and research, including consultations with organization development specialist Juli Lynch and input from the various people involved, I shifted my priorities. In the interest of expanding awareness of the Master Herder model and the Power of the

Herd skills, I decided to downsize my Arizona operation to open up more time and funds for writing and travel. Among other things, this meant selling some land, reducing my herd from fifteen horses to eight, and cutting some staff hours — all culling-related activities.

The hardest part for me was choosing which horses to keep and which to find new homes for. One of my favorites, a handsome Appaloosa named Sage, had come to live with me as a yearling twelve years earlier. This solid, intelligent gelding *loved*, more than anything, to be ridden, and he would get cranky and depressed if he didn't hit the trails regularly. Since my schedule didn't allow me much time to saddle up and head for the hills, I was *paying* a staff member to keep him happy in this regard. My colleague Shelley Rosenberg, on the other hand, specialized in teaching riding and had been Sage's primary trainer for a number of years. The two of them made a perfect match, though it was hard to hold back the tears when he stepped onto her trailer and into a new life.

Over nine months, other valued horses left us, two through connections with clients who adopted them. Finally, and most grievously, I lost my soulful ex-cow-horse El Dia to a deadly bout of colic (just as I had lost his predecessor Noche a decade earlier). At over thirty years old, El Dia was over ninety in human years, but the decision to euthanize him was painful, and the empty space he left in my heart substantial.

At the same time, it was a joy to see Spirit's mate Panther, a mustang, and their daughter, Artemis, excel in equine-facilitated learning activities. These horses were not particularly interested in being ridden. What's more, they exhibited a talent for working with people who had little or no equestrian experience. Panther and Artemis joined the by-then-experienced Spice Girls as the "staff members" most likely to inspire leaders of the future, with Indigo Moon, Orion, and Spirit himself excelling at teaching people how to work effectively with dominant personalities.

As I managed the Predator's sometimes-difficult task in this situation, the essential steps were to take *time* to cull my herd, to keep their talents and welfare in mind, and to assess which two- and four-legged staff members were most enthusiastic about the company's new direction. In the process, those who stayed strengthened and deepened their commitment to the work, as others were supported in finding their own greener pastures. If I had employed the Predator role without balancing individual and group needs, or if I had waited too long to engage it, the suffering would have far outweighed the benefits — and inevitable obligation — of using this sometimes-destructive yet necessary form of power.

## Back to Nature

I grew up in Youngstown, Ohio, a major hub of the steel industry. And I remember, even though I was only sixteen at the time, the crushing force of fear and despair that followed what people in the region still refer to as Black Monday. On September 19, 1977, the Youngstown Sheet & Tube Company announced shutdowns and massive layoffs at their Campbell Works, setting off a chain of events that sacrificed over ten thousand jobs by 1981. Thousands more jobs in supporting and related businesses were also lost. People working in construction, railroading, foundries, and steel fabrication suddenly found themselves with too much time on their hands and not enough food on the table.

The fallout from this event conjured up strange paradoxes. To the generations of locals who had thrived since the Industrial Revolution, the perpetual dark cloud over Youngstown was a sign of success. Two days after any big winter storm, the snow would turn light gray, a thin layer of soot glistening under the soft sheen of a perpetually compromised sun. In the early 1980s, as the steel industry disintegrated and waves of depression took hold of the population, the snow became whiter and the sky became bluer. Over the next thirty years, nature reclaimed the metallic landscape, scattering wildflowers over the carcasses of old foundries and railroad lines. Oaks, maples, and fruit trees pushed through the windows of crumbling factories as deer grazed on flowing grasses in the shadow of indecipherable old billboards and once-gleaming corporate signs.

It's still astonishing to me that an industry so lucrative and powerful could die so quickly. In early childhood, I was absolutely terrified of the mills, which were never far from view. Each day, as my mother drove my father to a local architectural firm, I watched from the protection of my tiny car seat as men and machines engaged in a brutal form of alchemy. Flames from the blast furnaces crackled and exploded ten stories high, casting an unholy light across miles of intricate ductwork spilling from the factories like the exposed entrails of some titanic beast. Though I was more fascinated than afraid of the smoke and all that fire, memories of those iron bowels would haunt my dreams. I would wake up, gasping for air, imploring my parents to do something about the writhing maze of pipelines that came to suffocate me in the night.

The area's first blast furnace was built in 1803. After Youngstown Sheet & Tube's collapse in 1977, it took only five years to demolish a steel town behemoth that had been gathering force for 174 years. How was this possible? According to some commentators, it was a remarkably efficient, unintentionally deadly team effort. In an online essay accompanying historic Youngstown photos, the author writes:

> Who killed Youngstown's steel industry? Quite frankly, it killed itself through suicidal self-interest. Steelmakers treated workers poorly and gave rise to combative unionism and a loss of corporate self-determination. The companies then failed to invest in modernizing their facilities. Steelmakers and city officials also fought to prevent other materials industries, such as manufacturers of aluminum and plastic, from coming to Youngstown. They would have diversified the city's steel-dependent economy. The United Steelworkers, buoyed by victories over working conditions and decent pay, continued their demands and strikes until they were paid better, on average, than other industrial laborers. Meanwhile railroads fought

Congressman Michael J. Kirwan's lake-to-river canal that would have given Youngstown's mills lower-cost transportation of coal, iron ore and limestone.

Suicidal self-interest, blind territorialism, and combative factions within companies and the community as a whole: That's what you get when Predators rule the land. As humanity habitually ignores evolutionary principles of balance, nonpredatory power, and mutual aid, nature sometimes loses its ability to support life; other times, it returns with a vengeance. Either way, hard-working, well-meaning people suffer in the intervening years of death and recalibration. Maybe, just maybe, we'll learn how to collaborate with natural forces that have been silently sustaining us, teaching us all along how to use the Predator role artfully and sparingly, rather than fall prey to its rabid, two-legged incarnations.

# PART III

# Balancing the Roles

# CHAPTER EIGHT

# Growing Pains

If any city deserves a second chance, it's Youngstown, Ohio. Despite its heavy industrial orientation, the city simultaneously produced conservationists who created a stunning urban nature preserve *in 1891*. The first of its kind in Ohio, Mill Creek Park still encompasses nearly three thousand acres of glacier-carved gorges, waterfalls, lakes, forests, and meadows. Public and private funds support a related environmental education center, scenic recreation facilities, and a horticultural wonderland of flowering fruit trees, roses, crocuses, daffodils, tulips, and exotic plants. Fellows Riverside Garden is a popular site for wedding photos, of course, but it also provides a serene haven from the daily worries of a steel town in transition.

The city was less inclined to create a lively art scene. Even so, Youngstown established a respectable regional symphony in the 1930s. This in turn inspired award-winning school music programs in the surrounding suburbs. My high school orchestra actually won a national contest that took us to Washington DC's Kennedy Center, though at the time, I didn't quite grasp what an honor it was to play there.

When people recount the sad story of Youngstown's downfall, they rarely mention these and other life-enhancing features — efforts that are still more impressive because they *prevailed* despite a depressed

economy and a dwindling population. Though I, too, left after gradu-
ation — working in Florida, moving to the Arizona desert, and subsequently traveling around the world — I still love visiting my hometown.
It's a bittersweet experience, one that nonetheless grows more hopeful
with each passing year. Remnants of crumbling steel works dot the
landscape like ancient Mayan ruins. But the city is especially stunning
in spring and fall precisely because of the natural wonders that were so
artfully preserved.

At the same time, I'm proud to see that, slowly but surely, industry
is returning to the region, bolstered, I hope, by wisdom gleaned from
tragic circumstances.

## Fragile Renewal

For this reason, I was especially excited to find that one of the people
who graduated from my Arizona-based facilitator-training program
(which attracts professionals from six continents) lives in Youngstown.
Even more intriguing, Gwendolyn Samuels is working in the steel
industry as she is building her business in the field of equine-assisted
learning.

The challenges of economic renewal didn't come up during Gwen's
original apprenticeship in 2013. But when she returned in 2015 for additional training in the Master Herder skills, lightbulbs seemed to go
off in her head daily as we discussed the unproductive behavior arising
when people overemphasize certain roles.

Most insidious are managers who unconsciously cling to predatory
and/or dominant tendencies even as they try to incorporate the latest
research on emotional and social intelligence into company culture.

In conversations and emails, Gwen described to me several telling
examples, one of which occurred at a national sales meeting attended
by over 250 people.

"Our group president — let's call him 'Andy' — had unbelievable
recall and could remember practically every person's name in the room,
as well as his or her division," Gwen told me. "That day, he had all the

people in the room give their name, division, title, and number of years with the company. Then he picked two random people, and asked each of them to give the name and division of a person he pointed to."

That all sounded fine and good: a high-level leader modeling a skill associated with the Nurturer/Companion role. Andy, it seemed, not only valued individuals and called them by name, he was encouraging others to do the same thing. However, the situation got ugly when he subsequently employed this seemingly benevolent exercise for another, more sinister purpose. In the true tradition of all immature Dominants, the charismatic group president managed to use an activity designed to build trust and connection as a way to attack someone unexpectedly as a negative example for others.

"It was really shocking," Gwen revealed. "When Andy asked these people to give someone else's name and division, he emphasized that no one in the room was allowed to help or even speak during this time. John, one of the senior sales representatives, was caught giving a clue to help an individual who was being asked to answer. Andy made John come up to the front of the room and stand in a corner with his back facing the audience of his peers and coworkers."

It wasn't a joke. Andy's demeanor was stern, sarcastic, and demoralizing.

"He actually stated that if he had a dunce cap, he would make John wear *that* while standing in the corner," Gwen said. "I still can't believe John complied and that no one else objected. We were just too stunned, I guess. But how can you trust someone who would subject another professional to such humiliating treatment, especially for a minor infraction that was really about helping a coworker — during what we all initially thought was an effort on Andy's part to encourage everyone to get to know each other?"

## Daily Dysfunction in the Office

Gwen also described the day-to-day antics of other managers, which were less overtly aggressive and demeaning. But they could be profoundly unproductive nonetheless, especially when alpha-style team members overemphasized the Dominant role, pushing others too hard too soon, regardless of circumstance.

> I was working on a project with Trevor, a government official who had the ability to help get our product on a state Qualified Products List. He agreed to get a feel for his upper management's take on our request and do what he could to help us out. Knowing that it would take some time, he asked for our patience while he worked on it.
>
> Part of my job responsibility in marketing is to build a working relationship with those who can help get our product approved in order for our salespeople to actually sell the product. I spoke with Rick, our sales representative for that state, explained the situation, and asked that he give us time to work through the process. I explicitly told him that if he pushed, we could get shut out.

Within a half hour, however, Rick did in fact pressure Trevor by sending him a presumptuous email. As expected, Trevor pushed back, telling Rick and Gwen that their company would now have to wait. "To make matters worse," Gwen reported, "this happened during an election year when the administration changed from Democrat to Republican. It takes a long time to get anything through the government bureaucracy with someone on your side, and even longer when they are offended. Although Trevor is still employed with the government, his superiors changed. I'm now in the process of rebuilding not only my relationship with Trevor, but also attempting to build a relationship with the new administration."

Despite a host of similarly frustrating experiences, Gwen told me that understanding the benefits and challenges of the five Master Herder roles immediately helped her function more effectively, even though she's currently the only one at work who has this information. "The first week I returned, it was like someone had turned a light on in the room. All of a sudden, I could make sense of previously confusing dynamics, and I didn't take dysfunctional behavior personally."

This in turn helped Gwen to stay poised and focused enough to work on solutions, rather than overreact to unbalanced leadership styles and instinctual power plays. She had more compassion for her colleagues, even those who acted aggressively, which allowed her to experiment with ways of working with them more effectively, rather than reject them as mean or hopelessly defective.

In particular, Gwen realized that some of the steel industry's most insidious difficulties arose from people who were "stuck in the Predator role."

"We deal with lots of acquisitions and mergers," she said. "When companies combine forces, certain high-level staff members have to cull members of departments that overlap. You start out with two accounting departments, two HR departments, and so on, and certain positions become redundant. Hopefully, these cuts are made thoughtfully and respectfully. But afterward, the same people who made these cuts continue to hold on to the Predator role after it is no longer useful."

This phenomenon creates a culture of competitiveness, territorialism, and aggression *within* departments and the company as a whole. In particular, the predatory inclination to use others' vulnerabilities against them, and to cull people who simply need additional training and support to excel, puts everyone on the defensive. No one knows who to trust.

In his 2002 bestseller, *The Five Dysfunctions of a Team: A Leadership Fable*, Patrick Lencioni emphasizes that issues related to coworker vulnerability seriously compromise a potentially high-functioning staff. In this sense, we're not talking about the physical vulnerability we would experience encountering a mountain lion while jogging down an isolated desert trail. We're talking about that psychological vulnerability people seem equally reluctant to face, even though they're not literally in danger of injury or death. The vulnerabilities Lencioni cites include "weaknesses, skill deficiencies, interpersonal shortcomings, mistakes, and requests for help."

His understanding of *trust* is also enlightening, especially for those working in innovative fields. Even in the most mundane, business-as-usual scenarios, the importance of this concept is significant: "Trust lies at the heart of a functioning, cohesive team," Lencioni writes. Yet most people mistakenly evaluate trustworthiness as "the ability to predict a person's behavior based on past experience."

This limited definition creates a major block to building emotional and social intelligence. It's a catch-22: Coworkers who display unproductive or even destructive behavior can't change their ways without further unnerving colleagues who want people to act predictably in order to trust them! To make matters worse, well-meaning staff members who crave structure and predictability are often unable to tolerate feeling vulnerable without going into a serious fight-or-flight mode, alienating coworkers in the process. Adding to the difficulty, *people with a low tolerance for feeling vulnerable often feel justified in using others' vulnerabilities against them*, especially in a predatory power system — sometimes by deriding supervisors and coworkers secretly behind their backs, sometimes by shaming them publicly, creating labyrinths of confusion, betrayal, and mistrust in all possible directions. All of these beliefs and behaviors become serious hurdles in changing old habits, learning new interpersonal tools, mending past difficulties, and getting back on task.

Lencioni emphasizes, "In the context of building a team, trust is the confidence among team members that their peers' intentions are good, and that there is no reason to be protective or careful around the group. In essence, team members must get comfortable being vulnerable with one another." To even imagine taking such a risk, however, people must "be confident that their respective vulnerabilities will not be used against them." This goes against legitimate survival impulses we develop in many business, educational, and social settings where predatory dominance remains the rule rather than the exception. "Achieving vulnerability-based trust is difficult because in the course of career advancement and education, most successful people learn to be competitive with their peers, and protective of their reputations. It is a challenge for them to turn those instincts off for the good of a team, but that is exactly what is required."

In *The Power of the Herd*, I address this challenge by offering procedures for helping people exercise a progressively higher tolerance for feeling vulnerable without becoming defensive (chapter 17). At the same time, I recommend that leaders create a culture where no one is rewarded for using others' vulnerabilities against them. In fact, it's important to state this publicly and, if possible, to make it a part of written employee evaluation forms. This way, people who unconsciously or intentionally engage in this trust-destroying practice are supported and, over time, required to change their behavior. Finally, I outline a process for developing the emotional heroism needed to face our fears, acknowledge our shortcomings, and diffuse extreme conflict (chapter 23).

Over time, I also realized that helping individuals to employ a balance of the Leader, Dominant, Nurturer/Companion, and Sentinel roles in their *nonpredatory forms* was essential. Otherwise significant dysfunction arises in all kinds of confusing ways. In studying modern human behavior through the lens of the Master Herder perspective, I have noticed that unproductive results occur even when people are proficient at three of these roles, particularly when one of those roles involves the Predator.

## Triple Threats

At the time I was writing this chapter, promotional trailers for the newly released film *Steve Jobs* asked a simple question: "Can a great man be a good man?" My reaction was to challenge our current definition of "great."

Jobs was a visionary who, as many commentators have observed, *let nothing stand in his way*. By shrewdly combining the roles of Leader, Dominant, and Predator, he intimidated, alienated, and sometimes outright betrayed colleagues, friends, and family members. Wielding a double-edged sword of single-minded ambition, he made sometimes-creative, sometimes-devastating decisions that won, then lost, Apple millions of dollars. At one point, Jobs even lost his own job with Apple and had to win it back. While his comeback was admirable, and his influence undeniable, he was an unbalanced, incomplete model of "ultimate success." If someone sacrifices goodness in their reach for greatness, then they will fall short, no matter what fame and riches they achieve.

A truly great person *must* be a good person, or he or she leaves a swath of pain, confusion, and *unnecessary* destruction behind that people who value freedom should neither tolerate nor emulate. In any worthwhile endeavor, experimentation must take place, and so mistakes will be made. Some efforts must be nourished, while other things must be culled. But a visionary leader must also respect, empower, and negotiate with others or he or she becomes little more than a dictator with a good idea.

Ambitious men and women are most likely to embrace the same power triumvirate that Jobs employed with such calculating efficiency: that age-old habit of emphasizing skills associated with the Leader, Dominant, and Predator roles, while neglecting the Nurturer/Companion's compassionate interpersonal genius and the Sentinel's steadfast, noble guardianship. As such, many people lauded as contemporary success stories are simply pharaohs and conquistadors dressed up in Armani suits: visionaries striving to build the next great architectural wonder, explore new territory, or search for gold at the expense of thousands of serfs and "common" workers.

Gangs and terrorists emphasize a slightly different trio, again by suppressing the Nurturer/Companion role. In this case, however, the innovative functions of the Leader are replaced by the surveillance capabilities of the Sentinel role, which, when combined with the instinctual power plays of an immature Dominant, and the cruel, mindless consumption of a unbalanced Predator, wreaks havoc in countless clever yet somehow still primitive ways. Even when employing the latest technology, this archaic perspective lacks a true visionary element. Since this particular combination reliably results in a high percentage of untimely deaths for those who employ it, you have to wonder why it still seems so strangely popular in subcultures throughout the world.

## Recovery from Abuse and Extreme Trauma

Over the last two years, I've learned that the ability to combine all five roles is not only helpful in business and educational environments, it's absolutely essential in working effectively with survivors of abuse and violent crimes.

Dr. Rebecca Bailey is a leading family psychologist, personal therapist, and abduction / family reunification specialist. Coauthor (with Elizabeth Bailey) of the book *Safe Kids, Smart Parents: What Parents Need to Know to Keep Their Children Safe*, she is frequently called upon as an expert commentator on CNN, *Good Morning America*, and other national news shows, such as those hosted by Anderson Cooper, Diane Sawyer, Piers Morgan, and Katie Couric. The founder of Transitioning Families, Dr. Bailey has worked with police departments and the FBI to raise awareness of and sensitivity to the issues that victims of rape, abduction, and other crimes face in reuniting with their families and healing over time. While she has worked with hundreds of individuals and families in crisis, she is best known as the therapist who helped Jaycee Dugard reunite with her family after Jaycee was rescued in 2009 from a highly publicized eighteen-year abduction in California.

I highly recommend reading Jaycee's memoir, *A Stolen Life*, to understand the multifaceted issues involved in healing from extreme experiences, including an in-depth look at the effective combination of office and equine-facilitated sessions she undertook with Dr. Bailey. These therapeutic interventions helped Jaycee and her family cut through the insanity surrounding them in the weeks and months after her highly publicized rescue from the man who abducted her, a time in which the press was acting in predatory ways as well.

On Dr. Bailey's part, the ability to moderate the journalistic feeding frenzy alone involved a strong yet thoughtful and compassionate combination of the Sentinel, Dominant, Nurturer/Companion, and

Predator roles. To insure the family's ongoing safety and to protect the privacy of Jaycee, her children, her mother, Terry Probyn, and other family members, the psychologist also had to teach her clients how to deal with law enforcement and also how to handle the press, which can further traumatize survivors in high-profile cases. At the same time, everyone involved had to exercise emotional heroism in processing the horrific experiences that occurred during Jaycee's kidnapping and Terry's tireless, eighteen-year search for her daughter.

Finally, Dr. Bailey, Jaycee, and Terry all stepped into an innovative leadership role in creating the JAYC Foundation, which offers support to crime survivors and their families, as well as educational programs for law enforcement and social service personnel nationwide.

Dr. Bailey contacted me after reading *The Power of the Herd*. While she appreciated the book's emphasis on social intelligence, leadership, and community-building skills, she was particularly intrigued by the concept of *nonpredatory power*. "The people I work with have dealt with some of the most vicious, self-serving human predators out there," the psychologist told me. "Victims of predatory acts often have trouble reclaiming their own power because they refuse to adopt the cruel and manipulative images of power their perpetrators modeled — and rightly so."

Dr. Bailey immediately recognized that seeing the horse not as a prey animal but as a nonpredatory power animal that draws on the wisdom and support of the entire herd offers trauma survivors and their families a metaphor for a new way of being successful in the world.

Horses work together to stand up to predators and protect vulnerable family members. Then, after the danger has passed, they all go back to grazing, back to enjoying life to its fullest. There's no question that humans in crisis can learn a lot from the courage, agility, and peaceful engagement with life that horses embody.

In subsequently working together with survivors of abductions and other extreme experiences, Dr. Bailey and I observed that deep healing happens most efficiently through nourishing relationships — through families and other caring social groups in which people are valued for who they are as individuals — and also through knowing that their loved ones are capable of supporting them during the hard times, celebrating the good times, and fostering an underlying sense of connection, rejuvenation, and exploration in daily life.

"Survivors need to define themselves by who they *are*, not what they went through," Dr. Bailey emphasized in a press release for a workshop she and I cofacilitated. "The scars of serious trauma can hold people back or become something they build upon and incorporate into new strengths. But people don't get better in a vacuum. This is definitely what brought Linda and I together: An understanding of the interdependent nature of life and, consequently, healing. From this perspective, it becomes clear that families, communities, and other social systems can promote growth and transformation — or reinforce fear, hate, resentment, and depression. Families are a lot like herds. They're impacted by each other, by the environment, and by the events that touch their lives. In order to help people move beyond challenging circumstances and thrive, you have to consider all the systems and their interplay. Giving people the support, and the skills, to reconnect to each other is crucial."

## Balance and Empowerment in Everyday Life

In 2013, Dr. Bailey and I created Connection Focused Therapy, a progressive skill-building modality designed not only to help individuals process trauma but also to give families the tools they need to handle crisis, uplift one another, and thrive long term. The Five Roles of a Master Herder are an important part of advanced work survivors do after initial therapeutic interventions.

We also lead trainings in this multidisciplinary model for therapists, social workers, educators, and equine-facilitated learning practitioners. While it takes time for professionals to develop proficiency in the horse-facilitated activities, we discovered that our students quickly generalize these skills to their own private lives.

Erin Menut, an Eponaquest instructor also trained in the Connection

Focused Therapy and Master Herder models, wrote to me that learning to teach these methods "really showed me where I was contributing to dysfunction in my own life by overemphasizing some of the roles and underemphasizing others. During my apprenticeship program, I began to chip away at this dysfunction and handle challenges in my life a lot better."

For example, Erin used these skills in negotiating with a highly dominant ex-partner who had a tendency to bully others into giving him whatever he wanted:

> Like a lot of women, I had been raised to behave in a Nurturer/Companion way — to forgive a lot, even when the other person didn't change his hurtful behavior — and to have no boundaries or very poor boundaries.
>
> I had ended the relationship by the time I came to Eponaquest in 2012, but I continued to have difficulties in dealing with my ex because he and I have a child together. I really had to take on the role of Sentinel to protect my daughter and myself: to keep watch over what was happening and how his behavior was harming us. I had to learn how to speak up, to set boundaries, and even use assertiveness, just to keep us out of harm's way. This is hard for a Nurturer/Companion! But for my daughter's sake, I found the courage.
>
> One of the best but most difficult things I learned was how to use dominance well in order to claim the space I needed to feel safe. While this was very uncomfortable for me, over time it has actually improved my relationship with my ex because I can just be very clear, rather than always trying to accommodate him, keeping silent and getting resentful, or getting drawn into endless, pointless arguments.
>
> I even use predatory power with my ex to cut off conversations that are only going to become arguments. I would also say I use predatory power on the inside to cull behaviors that are not productive. When my mind wants to get caught up in

the drama all over again, I have to tell myself to stop and cut off the energy that was going into that draining relationship, so that I can have the energy I want to enjoy my life, my daughter, and the horses. I tap into the visionary power of the Leader to imagine the life I want to lead and keep my mind focused on manifesting that, rather than getting continually dragged down into my ex's dominance games, or into discouragement, which is what had often happened in the past.

Things are much better now. By balancing the roles, I can keep moving steadily along with much more freedom and ease and enjoyment in my life — in my relationships, as a parent, and in my work. I am so grateful for the Master Herder teachings, and excited that I can now help others, who may have faced similar challenges, to balance the roles and find more joy in their own lives.

## School Days

The five roles also provide balance in educational settings. Charlotte Richardson, a seventh-grade general education and special education teacher, went through the Eponaquest apprenticeship program to learn how to employ horse-facilitated methods with at-risk children. In the process, she found that she could adapt many of the leadership and emotional/social intelligence skills to classroom activities, which excited her students because of the mere association with horses. Her principal was intrigued and subsequently supported Charlotte in teaching this material two periods a day, five days a week at Tucson's Challenger Middle School.

Over time, Charlotte found that the Master Herder skills were relevant to *her* overall effectiveness, no matter what subject she was teaching. Through conversations and emails, Charlotte told me:

In working with students with different needs and talents, I cannot stress how valuable it is to be able to fluidly choose between these roles throughout the day. My second-period class needs a healthy dose of the Nurturer/Companion to ensure they feel comfortable and safe. I have to constantly monitor the well-being of each student, more so than in any other class. Third period needs a Leader, someone to inspire them, but also to calm and focus them when they get overexcited!

Fourth and seventh periods, I work with the students chosen for my equine-facilitated learning program. This class has both special needs and general education students with incredible potential who call for me to be able to flow between the five roles from minute to minute. This class is full of potential leaders, some of whom are finding their way through tough home situations, self-harm, low self-esteem, high self-esteem, and ADHD.

My fifth-period class is my biggest challenge, requiring me to employ my least comfortable role: Dominant. These students also need me to use all the roles, but dominance is essential in setting firm boundaries, stopping unproductive behavior during group assignments, motivating "lazy" members, and handling passive-aggressive power plays. Students in the sixth period benefit from the use of the Dominant to deal with the behavior of half of the class and the Leader to inspire and draw in the other half of the class. On rare occasions, I have to employ the Predator when a student needs to be removed from class for their own and others' safety.

## Context Is Everything

Over time, like Charlotte, many people learn to excel at moving fluidly between the roles according to the setting. Each group and situation calls for a different balance among the five roles. This also means we must pay attention to each setting and how we respond. Just because we successfully balance the five roles in one arena doesn't mean we will automatically do so when circumstances change. For instance, when certain business or social systems encourage or even pressure people to overemphasize one or two roles, this can cause a reaction in which some individuals may abdicate the same roles in other situations.

Julie Bridge provides a classic example. As an Eponaquest instructor with advanced training in the Power of the Herd and Master Herder skills, Julie teaches this model to corporate and personal development clients, and she has become a keen observer of how she uses the different roles. Yet even she was unaware of certain imbalances in her own life until an eighteen-hand Thoroughbred with really bad manners, and the Master Herder assessment — which she thought she knew the answers to — illuminated some of these dynamics.

"Nokota, one of my rescued Thoroughbreds, was a bully, pure and simple," Julie wrote me. "Having become quite fluent at the Five Roles of a Master Herder, I could easily identify him as a Dominant, and an immature one at that. What troubled me to no end, however, were the out-of-the-blue attacks that would leave huge scars on his pasture mate, Brego, attacks which were becoming more frequent. Living with horses is akin to being inside of a living movie with all of your hidden issues blown up on the screen in Technicolor. I could not figure out what Nokota was trying to get me to see, but Brego was suffering the consequences of my cluelessness."

Several weeks later, Julie took the Master Herder Professional Assessment while serving as one of my cofacilitators at a leadership clinic. In discussing how different settings cause people to emphasize different roles, I emphasized that workshop participants needed to take the test with a *specific* professional setting in mind. While Julie also works as a senior sales director at a large company, she decided to focus on the challenges she was facing in heading a nonprofit specializing in equine-facilitated learning.

"I was sure that I already knew what the results would show: I was mostly Leader, secondarily Dominant, and Nurturer/Companion was somewhere in a distant third," she told me.

This *was* how she scored in the context of her corporate day job at a Fortune 500 technology company known for its somewhat predatory tendencies. "There I utilize a strong combination of leadership and dominance to change the way our sales reps interact with our customers," she confirmed. But Julie's leadership style turned out to be very different in her nonprofit organization:

> I stared at the paper for quite some time, questioning the scores I was looking at, relooking at the questions, adding up the scores again, and coming up with the same result. I was really, really off. Yes, I had scored high on leadership, but dominance was *dead last*. I found out I was more predatory than dominant and very high on Nurturer/Companion. I sat in a stunned silence — the kind of silence that takes hold when a person you thought you knew really well turns out to be entirely different than you thought. That person was me.
>
> I began to realize that this is what Nokota had been mirroring for me all along. It was not my corporate job that was suffering, but my own company where I struggled to compel some of my own staff to actually show up. That particular pattern for me had been growing into more and more of a problem through the year. I could not sufficiently staff the work I was doing with ongoing clients and larger workshops, and I soon understood that my inability to exercise dominance was the culprit.
>
> In my effort *not* to emulate my corporate day job, I had swung to the opposite polarity in my other business, and in doing so, I was overemphasizing the Nurturer/Companion to the point of distortion. Some of the very people I counted on to assist me had no issue giving me less than twenty-four-hours' notice that they would not be able to work after all. The more distorted the Nurturer/Companion became, the more and more I struggled with my own needs — and this put me squarely into the most unconscious, shadow aspects of myself. I may have gotten too far out in front at times, overemphasizing the Leader, but the real trouble came from the de-emphasis of the Dominant when it was needed most.

Upon returning to her California ranch, the dynamics between her horses began to change as Julie made conscious adjustments to the imbalances of her equine-facilitated practice: "The marks on Brego became fewer and fewer," she said, marveling. "I gave Nokota the permission and trust to become my main lesson horse, something that he really loves to do. And I began to strategically drive from behind when needed, without judgment and without shame — purely in a matter-of-fact manner to gain more commitment from my challenging staff and to find additional staff that reveled in the work. It was a profound realization that came from such an unexpected place."

## Seeds of Change

From Kabul to Paris to Moscow, Tokyo, New York City, and Youngstown, Ohio, people are suffering from the unbalanced practices of business leaders, politicians, bullies, and terrorists. Solutions are not easy, but change is possible. Recognizing that we already have the resources inside us is essential.

Learning to access and balance the Five Roles of a Master Herder is difficult to do by accident. But so is learning how to read and write. The first step in this case involves recognizing that you are *not* a Dominant, Leader, Nurturer/Companion, Sentinel, or Predator. You hold the seeds of all these roles merely by being human. Expand the vision of who you really are, support others in tapping a similar store of potential, gain inspiration from the benevolent side of nature, and life itself will provide plenty of practice.

The mosaics of power and connection arising from this effort will sustain — and uplift — us all.

# CHAPTER NINE

# Working with a Herd: Applications in Real Life

In mastering these multifaceted skills, it's helpful to understand why nomadic pastoralists developed proficiency in all five roles to live with herds of large, unfenced herbivores, a topic we explored briefly in chapter 2. But it's also enlightening to look at why some of our ancestors put down the hoe and followed their four-legged companions to begin with. Based on compelling evidence from ethnographic sources and the account of a pair of twenty-first-century naturalists, who experienced mutual transformation through encounters with another species, this plot travels so far afield from civilization's deepest-held beliefs about human superiority that it is, first of all, humbling in its implications. But it's also a hopeful story, one that offers modern leaders insight into how they, too, can gain the trust and cooperation of people who are both free and empowered — people who may be skeptical of anyone who tries to direct their behavior, let alone capture and corral them.

"Just as there was an age of exploration and an age of reason, the span from 10,000 BC through 2500 BC can be seen as the golden age of animal bonding," Meg Daley Olmert observes in *Made for Each Other*. "It must have been thrilling and dangerous, amazing and amusing, but none of these first tamers could have imagined just how completely these new relationships would change them, their world, and ours, forever."

In analyzing studies of nomadic pastoral tribes, Olmert discusses Dale Lott and Benjamin Hart's work on modern Fulani tribes in Africa (described in chapter 2). Their study, Olmert writes, "focuses not so much on the Fulani's amazing abilities to socialize their cattle, but on the socializing effect the cattle have had on the people who tend them. These humans have, according to Lott and Hart, become hybrids whose psyche is 'part and product of the behavioral properties of the cattle.'"

Something similar happened to naturalist Joe Hutto and his wife, Leslye, when a wild, female mule deer stepped courageously into their world and invited them into hers. Over seven years, the Huttos' views on life, nature, and animal intelligence expanded significantly as they developed an intimate relationship with the entire herd of mule deer, during which these two very different species learned to trust, educate, care for, and collaborate with each other.

Hutto, an Emmy Award–winning filmmaker and writer, chronicled these often-astonishing events in the 2014 book and accompanying PBS *Nature* documentary *Touching the Wild*. His goal was to share what he had learned about the secret lives of mule deer as he and Leslye forged ever-stronger relationships with multiple generations of these sensitive, unexpectedly brave, and intelligent animals. It's "hard to remember who I once was, and harder still to understand who or what I may have become," he admits. "My identity has undeniably been shaped and redefined by this community — this family into which I have in some strange way been assimilated."

Hutto inadvertently *lived* a process that may have resembled how ancient peoples came to form partnerships with the once-wild herbivores who eventually became the domesticated species we know so well. His experiences offer an important window into the mind-expanding, behavior-altering, sometimes heart-wrenching dynamics that may have led some of our ancestors to embrace the pastoral lifestyle.

As I compared Hutto's story with research on the human-animal bond and the habits of nomadic interspecies cultures, I recognized a compelling sequence of events. The Huttos' relationship with the first mule deer, and then with the herd, progressed through eight steps, which I describe in this chapter. For our purposes here, I am less concerned with whether this pattern is a valid, scientifically plausible theory on the genesis of nomadic pastoralism. Rather, the eight steps offer a deeper understanding of the Five Roles of the Master Herder in action — how they combine, evolve, and are balanced by a Master Herder. In essence, they reflect the process of how people can learn to connect with strangers who live by different rules. These same steps also reveal how social animals in nature employ and often combine the five roles. Most of all, the Huttos' experience with the mule deer exemplify why modern leaders must be willing to be transformed by those they propose to lead.

As you will see, this story of interspecies relations is directly relevant to those who would become better managers and teachers of humans. As you read, reflect on how employing these eight steps could enhance your effectiveness in your own various social settings. In particular, how might they help you collaborate with some of the wilder, more fearful, and more aggressive people we inevitably encounter along the way?

## Step One: Create an Oasis

Studies of ancient pastoral cultures suggest that herbivores were attracted to early agricultural communities and eventually enticed some of our more adventurous ancestors into a lifestyle based on moving with migrating herds. In turn, the nomads' intimate knowledge of animal behavior, combined with selective breeding practices, later made it possible for sedentary farmers to keep the much gentler descendants of these species close to home.

But we had to start small. Archeological records indicate that sheep and goats were loosely associated with humans around eleven thousand years ago, and they were fully integrated into settlements near Jericho around eight thousand years ago. Not everyone settled down, however. The Jewish culture, and hence the entire Judeo-Christian heritage, is based on tribes that chose to develop an increasingly sophisticated semi-nomadic lifestyle rather than accept the sedentary practices of some of their contemporaries. (For an in-depth discussion of the strong pastoral roots of the Jewish and Christian religions, see *The Power of the Herd*.)

After sheep and goats were domesticated, it took another thousand years for people to figure out how to work with the larger, fiercer ancestors of modern cattle, and it was over two thousand years after that before equines began living in close contact with humans. Once again, horses were initially associated only with nomadic cultures. It took a particularly bold and savvy group of people to not only observe but actually align with equine behavior, creating an interspecies culture based on equal parts freedom, power, and mutual aid. Still, it's important to realize that the increasing diversity of species associated with human settlements, and the increasing skill that early pastoralists developed in working with different animals, were both factors in forming partnerships with powerful herbivores like horses and cattle.

Long before our ancestors were capable of partnering with any of these animals, however, an attraction grew between humans and four-legged neighbors *who came and went as they pleased*. Moving from observation at a distance to hand-feeding and finally touch, the human-animal bond created a powerful feedback loop of increasing curiosity, respect, comfort, trust, and care. As Joe and Leslye Hutto's experience suggests, plenty of food, good cheer, and nonpredatory behavior would have surrounded the settlements most amenable to this process of mutual domestication.

The Huttos moved to Wyoming's Slingshot Ranch in May 2006, and they soon had the area around their house and barn exploding with life. The couple not only set up feeding stations and birdhouses, they began naming the wild residents and reaching out to them in ways that few ranchers bother to do. Joe and Leslye's interest in multiple species brought the shiest animals out of hiding. Tasty seeds may have been the initial attraction, but soon enough the farm pulsed with feelings of safety and celebration that must have radiated for miles.

As Hutto explains in his book: "We commonly sit on the front porch in the evening watching all the activity in the area with chipmunks scampering across our laps as they fill their cheek pouches and then diligently head to some secure location to deposit their stash — then back they come for another load. Naturally many of our chipmunks have names, and some will let me scratch them on their tiny heads while they shell sunflower seeds on the coffee table."

Hutto is also an experienced hunter, but he clearly doesn't over-identify with this role. Near the house, he and his wife soon created a small, stress-free, predator-free zone that protected more than their two horses. Even animals that many people would fear or reject as a nuisance were welcomed: "Like chipmunks, many of the bunnies have names and readily take horse cookies from Leslye's hand down at the barn....Leslye can call a name, and a pack rat will emerge from a hole in a log wall of the barn, walk out onto Leslye's lap, and casually take a horse cookie."

Even so, predators were not considered enemies. They were just barred from that small oasis that gave other animals respite from the sometimes-harsh realities of life. While appreciating the languid flights of large raptors from a distance, Leslye would chase eagles and hawks away from rabbits frolicking in the front yard. Still, when the couple found that a nearby kestrel nest was being bombarded by an overabundance of egg-loving bull snakes, Joe relocated a number of the ravenous serpents so that these delicate falcons could finally produce their long-awaited fledglings.

The ranch also grew alfalfa and other crops during the warmer months. Deer were invariably attracted to the back acres when they returned to the valley from summer migrations through high country, but the couple never expected to get anywhere near these inherently cautious herbivores, for good reason: When hunting season starts in the fall, rifle blasts echo for miles. In rural areas, Hutto reports, people living in trailers or houses on smaller acreage are known to shoot at deer passing through the yard at any time of the year, hoping to fill their freezers with venison from fortuitous, sometimes-illegal, kills.

Yet despite this constant threat, the mule deer visiting Slingshot Ranch proved to have keen, discriminating minds and a certain amount of courage. Like all intelligent, highly observant herbivores, they were capable of assessing the intentions of predators at a distance. Though smaller and more delicately boned than horses and cattle, the deer also sometimes succeeded in fighting off coyotes and wolves. A few of the adults were even strong enough to escape, and heal from, serious mountain lion assaults. Later, Hutto realized that does, who clearly recognize the voices of their own newborns, will answer the distress call of any fawn in the area, and they will often put their own lives at risk to thwart a predator's attack on someone else's child.

And so it happened that one particularly intelligent and gregarious doe became curious about the daily interspecies parties hosted by the Huttos, and she decided not only to stick around but to move closer to the real action down at the ranch house.

## Step Two: Observe While Being Observed

For many years, I secretly entertained the notion that wild herbivores may have been the ones to approach our ancestors, rather than the other way around.

This seemingly whimsical idea was finally confirmed when I read about Joe Hutto's experiences with the mule deer clan. Hutto hadn't set out to study this particular species. He and his wife, Leslye, instead found that a courageous doe was studying *them*, probably for quite some time before she gently made her presence known. One day, this unusually poised deer crossed the boundary between the ranch house and the surrounding wilderness, and she did something more amazing than step onto the property and gingerly sniff around: She stared unflinchingly into their eyes, something that herbivores are reluctant to do with animals they don't trust.

It happened in September, five months after the couple moved to Slingshot Ranch. Mule deer were just beginning to return from summer migrations, and the couple would watch them with binoculars from the porch as chipmunks skittered about looking for sunflower seeds and rabbits played nearby. One afternoon, Leslye looked out the kitchen window and saw a mule deer doe standing in the front yard. "As we gazed from the darker interior of the house," Hutto remembers, "the deer finally made eye contact.... We stood silent and motionless, certain that she would soon become fearful and the moment would be lost. However, to our amazement, she continued her obvious inquiry, which even included a quick halting step in our direction." Then she "slowly walked toward the back of the house and out of sight."

As the doe returned each afternoon, the Huttos began calling her Rayme (short for Doe-Ray-Me). She was so inquisitive that the couple assumed she must have had some previous contact with humans, but none of the other local ranchers and residents had ever heard of a mule deer being raised or fed by anyone in the area. Still, any deer's curiosity might have been piqued by the Huttos' two horses munching peacefully on high-quality feed near the house. Rayme probably first wandered among these gentle giants at night when the house was dark and quiet. Eventually, however, the Huttos realized she was doing something else out there, too.

> Rayme had this peculiar habit of staring at us through the window at night. We have thermal blankets that roll down over the cabin windows for really cold nights, but with the nearest neighbor half a mile away, in one hundred years, there had never been a curtain hanging on a window at the Slingshot. As a result, we live in something that must resemble a fishbowl as we walk through the well-lit house at night. Although a little disconcerting, we eventually realized that Rayme would literally follow us as we moved through the house, going from window to window, fascinated with our activities. At 10:00 PM you would look into the otherwise black square of a window and suddenly make out the face of a deer, almost pressed against the glass — there was Rayme — wide-eyed and watching our every move.

During the day, Rayme's interest was further piqued as she watched rabbits and squirrels around the house. These notoriously fragile, nervous animals not only played near humans but were groomed and hand-fed by the oddly compelling two-legged creatures.

As Dale Lott reported in his national park study, people think highly of others who are trusted by wild animals. Other species probably develop the confidence to approach us for similar reasons. The chipmunks, pack rats, and deer orbiting around Slingshot Ranch weren't just observing *human* behavior, they were taking cues from the comfort and safety that other animals, including the horses, exhibited in the Huttos' presence. If Joe had been using food to lure rabbits out of the brush to trap or shoot them, the outcome would have been different.

I've noticed that my association with horses in particular has a similar effect, even though horses aren't wild animals. When I'm out riding, herds of mule deer in Arizona continue grazing and even step forward with curiosity as we meander along the trail. They don't show the same level of comfort when I'm hiking on foot. Back at the ranch, when I sit quietly with the herd, rabbits, squirrels, and birds will come within a few feet of my chair, even though I don't have food with me, and I'm not trying to entice them in any way. This trust is extended to strangers who show a similarly calm, respectful demeanor: When the horses and I are working with small groups of equine-facilitated learning clients, rabbits sometimes approach and even sit under trees to watch us.

It doesn't take much imagination to see the human parallels. How any new leader handles the initial "observation" period is crucial to building trust and cooperation with employees, colleagues, clients, vendors, and/or constituents. A beefy résumé, an intriguing plan of action, and a slick or inspiring speaking style may win someone an influential job in the first place. But particularly in entrepreneurial, community-based, and diplomatic settings — where stakeholders may be a bit more flighty and are truly free to stay or leave — every move this person makes *communicates*.

If, like the Huttos, leaders set up an oasis where diversity is appreciated and predatory behavior is minimized, people will begin to relax. This may require employing the Dominant role to stand up to aggressors and discourage overly competitive people from using co-workers' vulnerabilities against them. It's also important to engage the Nurturer/Companion role to gain trust and discover individual needs, talents, and perspectives. In this effort, it's helpful to occasionally connect with individuals and small groups in an agenda-less, open-minded, openhearted setting — and, in turn, to reward people for stepping out of their hiding places, not with sunflower seeds, of course, but with feelings of delight and interest.

Employing the Sentinel role allows new leaders to evaluate group dynamics in relation to the company's mission, strengths, and challenges. This in turn results in thoughtful policy and organizational changes that inspire employees to cooperate, and, over time, to excel. Using the Sentinel role with nonpredatory intent also insures that any decision to cull programs or lay off workers arises from an informed and compassionate use of the Predator role.

Finally, as the Huttos discovered with their wildest of neighbors, it may be beneficial for new executives to sometimes go about their daily business in full view of others, even if it feels a bit like working in a fishbowl. Then again, studies have shown that workers must also be able to minimize distractions to excel, so finding a balance between transparency and privacy is key to effective leadership.

These simple, yet often-counterintuitive acts won't necessarily win everyone over. But they will attract the attention of staff members who truly care about the organization's well-being. These same people often hold unofficial leadership roles and are, for any number of reasons, respected and trusted by others. Once a new manager gains the confidence of these informal ambassadors, other, more reticent or jaded members of the herd will quite naturally follow.

## Step Three: Welcome the Ambassadors

As Rayme casually wandered into the Huttos' yard each day, her family group began browsing the vicinity. Leslye and Joe started tossing horse cookies out to the doe, who stayed close by when they stepped onto the porch. "Soon Rayme became a familiar resident around the house, and we discovered that all we needed to do was walk outside and say, 'Rayme!' and she would mysteriously appear within seconds."

In a matter of weeks, Rayme's entire herd felt comfortable entering the yard. Soon enough they were given names, too. Several of the otherwise healthy deer showed signs of narrow escapes from predatory attacks. Notcha, "a profoundly beautiful and elegant deer" who showed "a particular affinity for Leslye," was named for "a distinct notch taken out of her left ear." Charm, a yearling doe, was named for the "black scars that girdled both her lower front legs, like bracelets, just above the hooves. Her entire body was covered in large, dark patches and lines from obvious scarring. She must have been horribly mauled by coyotes or a mountain lion when she was a fawn, but miraculously survived."

By late November, several bucks arrived on the scene. They accepted the presence of humans even more quickly, in part because the does were comfortable with Hutto and his wife, but to a larger extent because the males had something else on their minds.

> Rutting mule deer bucks, although profoundly wary most of the year, can become almost oblivious to humans when preoccupied with prospective mates. If you are standing twenty feet from twenty does and fawns in the first week of December, the biggest buck may pass close enough to touch you, offering only a nervous glance and a canted ear that dismisses your odd and inconvenient presence.

A particularly large and impressive male the couple named Daddy Buck "immediately identified us as safe neighbors and in a few days became entirely comfortable with our presence." On occasion, they offered him some "high protein supplemental food" when he appeared especially "starved and exhausted" from his amorous adventures.

Over time, it occurred to Hutto that mule deer who survived beyond their first year were *warriors*. As he got to know multiple generations, he could see that youthful innocence and optimism were all too often replaced by a profound sadness in their eyes. When one of the herd leaders died of an unknown illness, her family camped out near the body for more than a week. Other deer, clearly traumatized by their own close calls with predators, were tenacious survivors and overcame outrageous injuries, no doubt through the opportunity to heal near the house. The naturalist also observed several instances where a mother would guard the remains of a fawn killed by a mountain lion. Though these does couldn't save the lives of their children, they grieved the loss for days, and some successfully kept coyotes and vultures away from the body.

Not all carnivores, Hutto discovered, exhibited the behavior of predators designed by nature to keep life in balance. Like human trophy hunters, some were fetishists. As he reported with some disgust, at least one of the large cats in the area had a habit of eating only the liver and whatever flesh it took to get to this tasty treat before wandering off to find the next organ donor. Over their seven-year association with the deer, Hutto could see that the careless and constant two-legged and four-legged assaults on the mule deer were decimating the population, and his heart went out to these gentle, deep-feeling creatures. *The safety zone* created around the ranch house may therefore have been *more attractive to Rayme than the promise of food.*

It didn't take long for the Huttos to realize that mule deer do not live on grass alone, not even close. A complex array of social relationships and mutual aid sustained them. The ability of this particular herd to discern that a couple of trustworthy humans lived in the area was also critical to the tenuous survival of several orphaned fawns and to the larger herd's ability to enjoy life at times.

Was Rayme a visionary among mule deer? The results of the contact she initiated certainly suggest it. Her innovative association with the Huttos saved the lives of numerous deer over the years by introducing her much more wary herd members to an oasis of rest and renewal.

Rayme's actions also may impact the long-term viability of her herd, since she came upon a writer and film producer capable of giving her family a *voice.* Hutto's stunning words and images may finally bring enough public attention to the plight of Wyoming's mule deer population at the eleventh hour. At the very least, the book and documentary may discourage hunters who truly care about conservation from shooting does and fawns during still-legal seasons. When does are killed, the vast majority of fawns also die as a result of losing their mothers.

"For reasons that will always remain a mystery, Rayme found us — Rayme sought us out," Hutto marvels. And she stayed just long enough to build the foundation of what would become a fruitful interspecies relationship.

After that first magical winter at Slingshot Ranch, Rayme and the rest of the deer migrated to their summer range in May. The Huttos thought that the herd might return to their wary ways and lose the thread of trust they'd established, seemingly miraculously, because of an unusually intelligent and gregarious doe. But the following fall, the deer returned, and after only a few hours, they were once again comfortable with the couple.

> Clearly, the new fawns judged from their mothers' demeanor that even though we were a strange curiosity, we must be a relatively safe curiosity. Their behavior was distinctly different from the fawns we had met the previous year. In fact, the new, wide-eyed fawns were so accepting of us that it was hard to avoid the improbable suspicion that they had received some prior instruction on what to expect.

After many weeks waiting for Rayme, however, Hutto "sadly concluded" that she had not survived:

> I still regret not getting to know her better, for clearly she was extraordinary. She had bridged the divide between her family and ours, and all that has transpired is her lasting legacy. Rayme was something of an oracle who voluntarily brought a message that merged one universe with another — she was the one who so generously and unexpectedly chose to share

her unique vision of the world. Rayme opened a door I never knew existed.

Opening doors, making connections, seeing potential in people or animals that the average "herd member" rejects as strange and suspect, these skills come easily to ambassadors like Rayme. It may be a talent or perhaps a perspective developed through a rare confluence of life circumstances — most likely a combination of both. In analyzing what makes these unique individuals tick, I was initially tempted to add a sixth role to the Master Herder model to include them, yet this isn't truly necessary. Ambassadors actually combine three of the roles — Sentinel, Nurturer/Companion, and Leader — while somehow inspiring other group members to minimize dominant and predatory behavior. In their ability to take emotional as well as physical risks to connect with others, they are visionary warriors of the heart, and they seem to be the primary motivators of social evolution.

At their most innovative, ambassadors create the conditions for large populations to reach across cultural and species lines. More commonly, these gifted connectors go about their business in much less monumental settings. Recognizing, aligning with, and most importantly, *learning from* the ambassadors in any group gives savvy leaders a leg up in gaining cooperation and rallying the untapped talents of all kinds of people, including those who don't yet have the courage or social skills to communicate well and collaborate with others.

Unfortunately, as a result of overemphasizing dominant and predatory behavior, conquest-oriented cultures and businesses tend to ignore, or even malign, employees and community members who are functioning as ambassadors. A classic example is Melanie's story in chapter 5, about the low-performing programmer whose social skills were critical to a software company's productivity. To make matters worse, these people may not see themselves as leaders because of a marked unwillingness to claw their way to the top or intimidate others into submission. Some avoid promotion; others are repeatedly passed over when they do apply for managerial positions. When this happens, the organization as a whole suffers.

## Step Four: Name the Individuals

In the 1990s, many of the equestrians I encountered believed that animals were incapable of thought and emotion. "It's all instinct," one of my trainers told me whenever I brought up anecdotal evidence to the contrary. Some of the local ranchers insisted that, unlike dogs, horses weren't smart enough to recognize their own names. Even when a Thoroughbred, quarter horse, Appaloosa, or Arabian had a registered name, it was considered a convenient way to link valuable breeding stock to their ancestors *on paper*. If a cowboy at one of these operations wanted someone to catch a few geldings in the back pasture, he'd distinguish them by color or marking, saying something like, "Hey, go get the black, the line-back dun, and that chestnut with the two white socks."

Over the years, I met a number of unregistered cow horses who had *never* been given names. I questioned this practice once, simply by mentioning that my mare came when I called her, and two grizzled ranch hands looked at each other, rolled their eyes, shook their heads, and smirked. "You feed her, don't you?" one asked. I nodded. "That's not her name working for you; that's her stomach," he replied. When I mentioned that horses are commonly taught vocal commands like "walk," "trot," and "giddy up," the other argued that this was "conditioning." Horses, these men insisted, weren't conscious enough to have an actual identity, and so naming them was superfluous, something that riders did for their own amusement.

Since that time, the popularity of the natural horsemanship movement has changed more than a few cowboy minds. Well-known, Stetson-clad clinicians travel the country introducing training techniques that take the mental and emotional fitness of both horse and rider into consideration. But the idea that a wild animal might respond to a name is still up for debate in many circles. Even the Huttos, who called pack rats out of hiding for hand-fed treats, weren't sure that mule deer would be able to distinguish their names, especially after they left the ranch for summer grazing that first year. As the does returned the following September, however, Joe and Leslye were pleased that the deer not only remembered their two-legged friends, new fawns trusted the couple more quickly as a result.

As it became clear that Rayme had probably met with a tragic end, every doe that walked onto the property was cause for celebration. When Notcha arrived, the Huttos were thrilled and relieved. However, she was also traveling with some new companions. As these much more skittish deer caught sight of Joe standing in the yard, they turned in fear and began trotting toward the mountains. As Joe described:

> Leslye exclaimed through the glass, "Say her name! Quick." I called in a loud voice, "Notcha!" Then I repeated, "Notcha!" To our absolute astonishment, Notcha stopped and turned, staring momentarily, and, then, leaving the other deer, ran — yes, ran — at a gallop directly to me. We were stunned at the revelation that she not only recognized my voice and knew exactly who I was after six months without doubt, but, even more amazing, recognized her name! Following Notcha's example, the other deer soon joined us for a few minutes of casual greetings that included a few horse cookies. I returned to the house astonished. Why on earth would a wild deer have the capacity to so readily recognize and retain the oral association of some name that had been assigned to her in a previous year? I began to wonder how that particular kind of identification could be included in the deer's repertoire of social possibilities — and why. It was at that moment that I began asking a question that still haunts me: "Who am I actually dealing with here, and what *are* the possibilities?"

Even now, pastoral tribes are much more likely to name their animals than sedentary farmers. But this unexpected anecdote from the Huttos suggests that naming may have been an important part of the ancient bonding process that allowed herbivores and humans to trust each other, move together, and eventually live together.

Even though animals don't have the vocal capacity to name us, they appear to appreciate it when we name them. Perhaps in the act of naming, human beings break through a haze of skepticism, objectification, and anthropocentric self-absorption to recognize the unique qualities and potential of each and every individual.

Back in 1982, when mainstream scientists insisted that animals were unintelligent, purely instinctual beings, philosopher Vicki Hearne went through all kinds of intellectual contortions to challenge this mechanistic perspective. Her book, *Adam's Task: Calling Animals by Name*, feels a bit dated, especially in the wake of the Cambridge Declaration on Consciousness. But when Bazy Tankersley, founder of the respected Tucson breeding operation Al-Marah Arabians, introduced me to this book in the mid-1990s, I practically fell to my knees and wept tears of gratitude.

Hearne mixes anthropological, historical, and religious references with her own experiences as a dog and horse trainer. She argues that while we gained technological expertise through the process of civilization, we lost something important in distancing ourselves from other living beings. "Typography," a word she uses to describe humanity's tendency to generalize and categorize, "made possible further gaps between us and animals, because we have become able to give them labels, without ever calling them by name."

Over the centuries, we've generalized this practice to other humans as well. My colleague Juli Lynch said to me, "I've seen so much depersonalizing of people in organizations, even to the extent where someone is referred to by his job duty versus his name. I've worked with banks that had only thirty to forty employees, and the CEO did not know everybody's name — not because he couldn't remember that many names, but because it wasn't important to him. Employees knew it didn't matter to him. And guess what: The company's turnover rate was exceptionally high for a small-town employer where jobs were not easy to find."

The case for correcting this dehumanizing behavior becomes all the more poignant when you realize that calling an animal by name is important to forming effective working relationships with our four-legged friends. Unlike the cowboys I mentioned earlier, Hearne insists that "training horses creates a logic that demands not only the use of a call name…but also…the making of the name into a real name rather than a label for a piece of property, which is what most racehorses' names are." As the title of her book suggests, she believes that "deep in human beings is the impulse to perform Adam's task, to name animals and people as well." She emphasizes that we need to take this ancient art form seriously by choosing "names that give the soul room for expansion."

Hearne contends that naming our animal companions links us back to an earlier form of consciousness that modern humanity lost when we moved from oral tradition to writing or literacy. Linguistic anthropology, she reports, "has found out some things about illiterate peoples that suggest" they used "names that really call, language that is genuinely invocative," rather than our current culture's overemphasis on "names as labels." The author cites a lecture she attended with an anthropologist who was captivated by the "surprising" perspectives that certain "illiterate languages" reveal:

> One of his stories was about an eager linguist in some culturally remote corner trying to elicit from a peasant the nominative form of "cow" in the peasant's language.
>
> The linguist met with frustration. When he asked, "What do you call the animal?" pointing to the peasant's cow, he got, instead of the nominative of "cow," the vocative of "Bossie." When he tried again, asking, "Well, what do you call your neighbor's animal that moos and gives milk?" the peasant replied, "Why should I call my neighbor's animal?"

Ultimately, Hearne writes, she is "not arguing against advances in culture, only pointing out that it is paradoxically the case that *some advances create the need for other advances that will take us back to what we* call the primitive" (italics added). I would further emphasize that when early conquerors began to objectify, corral, and eventually enslave both animals and people, our literate civilization not only lost sight of the real power of naming, it relinquished the nomad's sophisticated understanding of *leadership through relationship*. This was knowledge that came directly from partnering with animals who maintained active social lives. Modern leaders all too often treat *people* more like machines than sentient beings. In this respect, civilization has "evolved" in an unproductive direction. Resurrecting the knowledge of ancient pastoralists is crucial to shifting this demoralizing trend.

This becomes especially clear in studying the Huttos' example. Joe and Leslye didn't scientifically *habituate* a *herd* of mule deer. The couple formed meaningful relationships with receptive individuals who initiated a level of contact they were comfortable with. As a result of the respectful, highly responsive behavior Hutto and his wife exhibited, they progressively gained the interest and trust of a wider mule deer network.

Far too many leaders try to amass power by controlling *groups* of people, but that only works with disempowered populations (people who relinquish their potential gifts through fear and mindless conformity). Forming alliances with free, intelligent, creative adults requires a different approach: cultivating an expanding network of relationships with individuals who are recognized — and valued — for their unique talents, skills, and personalities.

Rayme and Notcha represented the auspicious start of the Huttos' seven-year journey naming well over two hundred individuals with recognizable faces, markings, and distinct personalities. If Joe and Leslye had lived a few thousand years earlier, they may very well have left what would have been a primitive grain-producing settlement and followed their adoptive herd mates on summer migrations, swinging back around to the Slingshot Ranch valley just in time for fall harvest. In the process, the human element would have been in better position to protect the many does, fawns, and bucks who died due to accident or predation during those migrations.

In the lives of many twenty-first-century humans, an ancient pattern is once again repeating itself, calling attention back to an earlier curve in the great spiral of evolution, that time when *increasing mobility, freedom, and mutual aid* grew out of a fertile period of sedentary development. During that first cycle, times of plenty, boosted by prehistoric agricultural and technological innovations, provided food, water, safety, and camaraderie. This in turn encouraged some people to expand their horizons and collaborate with strangers who orbited around these settlements; strangers who were not shy about moving to greener pastures during heat, drought, and other compromising weather conditions.

Strangers like Notcha, who felt the sincerity of a tenuous attraction and became friends with people who reached out, recognized her uniqueness, and called her by name.

## Step Five: Nurture the Herd

In *Living with Herds: Human-Animal Coexistence in Mongolia*, Natasha Fijn effectively illustrates how deeply pastoral cultures care for their animals. Oxytocin's social recognition circuits cross species lines, creating, as Fijn discovered, a nature-based philosophy of equality.

The Mongolian pastoralists she encountered knew every animal by name. This, however, didn't affect their ability to make tough decisions. Rather, Fijn writes, it reinforced "an egalitarian outlook, without favoritism or treating the animal as the equivalent of a pet. Likewise the attitude within Mongolian herding society is to take care of everyone within the herding community, not just singling out individuals for special treatment. Nonetheless, contingencies such as extreme weather conditions, parental survival, and other factors do require that some animals have differential treatment from others." In particular, orphan foals, calves, and lambs are brought into the tent, bottle-fed, then released back into the larger herd when strong.

"Mongolians do not eat animals that are under one year of age," the author emphasizes. When she told one of the tribe members about the

Western practice of consuming lamb and veal, tears welled up in the woman's eyes as she quietly said, "We love our young animals, so we couldn't eat them."

"She must have thought it a strange practice," Fijn concludes, "as she was being so careful to nurture some weak lambs that were sleeping beside the hearth in front of her. It would be counter-intuitive for a herder to kill them and eat them before they had produced any young of their own, when the animals had not yet lived a full life. If a young lamb dies from weakness or illness, the herder then utilizes the hide but does not eat the meat." This reluctance to consume what our culture considers a delicacy shows how deeply bonded Mongolian herders become through the oxytocin-boosting activities of nursing and caring for the tribe's four-legged children.

Meg Daley Olmert emphasizes that oxytocin is "the *glue* that holds the herd and tribe together." In pastoral cultures, this is less about feeding the animals than caring for them in ways that involve a great deal of touch. Female cattle, sheep, goats, horses, camels, and even reindeer feed everyone at times, blurring the lines of oxytocin's supreme bonding power through the daily act of milking and being milked. The hormone's calm-and-connect effect releases feelings of relaxation and affiliation across species lines, lowering blood pressure and suppressing the fight-or-flight response. Women tend to handle milking and dairy production, but even male herders spend a good part of each day grooming and massaging their animals (who often initiate these encounters), causing both species to temper their fierceness with sensitivity and affection.

How did their ancient ancestors gain the ability to touch these sometimes-aggressive, potentially dangerous animals to begin with? Once again, Joe and Leslye Hutto illustrated how this might have happened, and their experience suggests it didn't take as long as you might think!

During the couple's first two years at Slingshot Ranch, various pioneering deer took risks that forged progressively stronger bonds between the two species. Rayme made the first overture. Notcha startled the Huttos by recognizing their name for her. And Charm's fawn, Little Possum, finally "breached the divide of physical touch," whereupon a number of other deer became amenable to being gently rubbed and scratched, leading still other deer innovators to introduce mutual grooming sessions with the humans.

A particularly gregarious wild doe named Cappy initiated contact with Joe within days of encountering her first human. She loved being groomed so much that she began making increasingly assertive requests for attention by pawing Hutto's backside if he walked away or ignored her. Joe was concerned this growing familiarity would make the deer more likely to approach humans who might shoot them. But Cappy's behavior quickly assured him that she remained discerning when it came to any two-legged creature she might encounter. Hutto noted, "Like the other deer, if a stranger neared the house, she was gone in a flash." Over time, Joe realized:

> Her ability to convey meaning to me in the form of some unspoken communication that was decidedly clear and complex suggested to me that I was now dealing with a creature of extraordinary potential — perhaps even the potential to reveal the more obscure and secretive nature of the mule deer, the innermost workings of personality, motivation, intelligence, and behavior. Cappy made it obvious if she thought danger could be near or if she was in need of a grooming session.

In successfully saving an orphan named Peep that same year, the couple began to grasp the truly life-saving power of touch and affection. When the fawn appeared at Slingshot Ranch, she was so weak and emaciated that Hutto didn't hold much hope for her survival. Though she began to rally with some high-quality feed, something crucial seemed to be missing.

> I realized that she was not just starved for food and merely tolerant of my touch; she was starved for both food and affection. Clearly, she had gone for many months without the attentions of her mother and was desperately touch-deprived. Late one

morning, in the comfort of the warming sun, I dropped on my knees and, with one arm across her chest, began grooming her with my hands about the head and neck. Only momentarily unsure about this close proximity and partial restraint, she suddenly went limp in my arms and appeared to fall into some sort of semiconscious torpor as I continued to gently scratch and rub her. It seemed as if her hunger for physical contact had also reached crisis proportions. Each day after a satisfying feeding session, I would hold Peep and [groom her]...but she would prevail on me for physical contact two or more times a day. Her need for affection seemed boundless.

Moments of wonder, inspiration, and connection abounded that winter. But Hutto subsequently found that his profound experiences "touching the wild" guaranteed that he was destined to be *touched* by the wild as well — and that involved more *emotional heroism* than he bargained for. Even as he "cheerfully bade" the deer farewell at the onset of that second migration season, Hutto admits that he "was naïve and had not yet learned that knowing — even loving — a wild mule deer was a double-edged sword — a sword that would open a secret world with one edge and pierce your heart with the other."

The oxytocin bond is the handle of that double-edged sword. It heightens social acuity and enhances name-recognition circuits, while boosting confidence, focus, trust, clarity, and learning capacity. But there's a highly motivating, sometimes-painful side to this endogenous, behavior-altering chemical: concern for the well-being of others.

Like Rayme the year before, Cappy did not return the following autumn, and the grief Hutto felt came in waves.

Even though Cappy is only one of two hundred such fragile relationships I have formed, rarely a day goes by that I do not think of her strangely beautiful, inquiring, gentle face and the unexpected vacuum she left in my life. But after all, I considered myself to be a hunter, a rancher, and an objective man of science — even once trained as a warrior — a man...fully resigned to the inculpable and even noble realities of life and death, and not to the childish mythology that life somehow favors and protects the living. In fact, it could be said that, at least to some extent, all living beings *persist* in spite of life, not because of it. Now this reality has come to define my life, as I am haunted by so many missing faces.

Hutto didn't count on connecting with the mule deer so easily. He didn't expect to grieve the loss of some of these relationships so deeply. Even so, the many ways in which the deer reached out to *him* add to growing evidence that the tendency to seek connection, and to offer as well as request mutual aid across species lines, is a part of nature, that "life" does, in fact, "favor and protect life." From this perspective, the human-animal bond is not a by-product of civilization or a contrived innovation; it is the *heart of evolution* in action.

A similarly painful yet transformational emotional connection may have been the deciding factor that motivated some of our ancestors to leave their fields and follow their four-legged friends. In the process, farmers and hunters became nurturers and protectors. Out on the range, people eventually discovered that milking a goat or cow or horse could sustain tribe members when there was nothing in sight but grass. Loose interspecies associations became vital, mutually beneficial partnerships. Along the way, pastoralists would have faced a more rigorous series of challenges as humans became fully integrated into the herd.

The mutual socialization of two- and four-legged animals is a much more ambitious proposition than touching and feeding a herd that comes and goes. The simple act of nurturing youngsters, for instance, can have dire consequences as increasingly powerful herbivores reach adolescence. This is why the Huttos, for instance, drew a serious line between their willingness to offer older orphaned fawns hay or grain and a reluctance to bottle-feed newborns.

That would invite human imprinting, and as a consequence, fawns would be confused about their own identities as individuals and as members of a species.... Many human-imprinted buck deer — especially whitetails — will predictably become aggressive toward humans, and even does on occasion become dangerous around children. The orphans we were able to rescue were somewhat older, starving fawns that were simply given supplemental food and thus a slightly improved chance for survival.

I'm inclined to disagree with Hutto slightly on one point. I know very well from experience that even domesticated horses who are bottle-fed can become dangerous as they reach adolescence, especially if caretakers try to relate exclusively through the Nurturer/Companion role. Still, the aggression doesn't seem to result from confusion of the animal's personal identity so much as a more intimate inclusion of humans as herd members, *a line all pastoralists cross*. Adolescent herbivores — and males especially — challenge siblings, parents, and other adults. If some of those herd members happen to be much smaller and lacking a couple of legs, well, so be it. Yet even without the more concentrated imprinting that bottle-feeding encourages, most young horses still experiment with ways to intimidate humans — and they should not be trusted with children, or with inexperienced adults for that matter.

As my stallion Merlin illustrated more dramatically than most, a few thousand years of selective breeding is no substitute for the proper socialization of *both* species. Domesticated equines can be extremely intolerant of people who lack a balanced understanding of power, people who either coddle and overindulge or aggressively restrain, confine, punish, and otherwise try to intimidate these animals into submission. Behavior that humans get away with among their own kind can be disastrous at the barn. Pastoralists would not have endured without the skills that modern civilization ignores.

To even survive their daily interactions with empowered herbivores, let alone keep the herd and the tribe together, ancient nomads had to move fluidly from the observant guardianship of the Sentinel role and the supportive connection of the Nurturer/Companion role to the much more active Leader and Dominant roles, which are capable of socializing rambunctious adolescents. To up the difficulty level, early pastoralists had to use all four of those roles in their *nonpredatory* forms or the entire herd would have run off. It is here, once again, that humans expanded their horizons by taking cues from their four-legged elders.

There are several clear lessons for modern leaders here: Authority figures should expect to be challenged, even in otherwise cooperative settings. Sometimes, well-meaning executives let more aggressive middle managers wreak havoc, with dire long-term consequences for the organization. Valuable employees who refuse to submit to such treatment will subsequently "run off," taking their talents elsewhere. At the opposite end of the spectrum, leaders who feel threatened by naturally powerful staff members will fire Dominants too quickly.

Challengers may need socializing, not culling. But it takes a savvy adult with Master Herder skills to help talented yet still "immature" people of all ages learn to master their own vast resources of power and potential.

## Step Six: Differentiate between Dominants and Leaders

In the book *Touching the Wild*, Hutto describes discovering the difference between dominance and leadership by watching the animals themselves, just as pastoralists must have done thousands of years ago. Even though the naturalist still uses terminology related to dominance, his descriptions of a doe who shows the classic characteristics of a leader are remarkably similar to what Mark Rashid and I observed in horses who also exemplify this role (see page 56).

As usual, it was easy for Joe and Leslye to recognize dominant bucks. For two years, a male they named Daddy Buck held this post. "We saw him pass by a third year, but he politely surrendered the area to a more dominant and imposing buck we named Moses," Hutto writes. "When three-hundred-pound Moses swaggered into the yard with head lowered and ears canted back, we were reminded of the Red Sea parting, as thirty-five deer respectfully moved far to either side."

It was a doe named Raggedy Anne that demonstrated the qualities of a truly accomplished herd leader.

In the midst of constant minor mule deer bickering and rancor concerning issues of status and hierarchy achieved through expressions of dominance and submission, we noticed that Anne was never the focus of these disputes, nor was she ever inclined to express any superiority toward any other deer. Gradually, as we came to recognize some of the more subtle communication that was unfolding around us, we observed, for example, that when Anne's space was being violated, she would simply look and raise her chin, and, without fail, the offending deer would acquiesce, moving away with barely a glance. It was clear that Anne was the dominant doe, the mild-mannered matriarch, the most humble queen, and for our first season with the deer, we had never known this to be the case.... With no need to reinforce her position of authority, she seemed almost passive and disconnected from the busy social activities around her. All does defer to all antlered bucks, but, still, throughout the winter months, the related bucks are inclined to follow the maternal herds. However, we always noticed that when the deer were on the move, it was usually Anne who would first begin walking away from the group with her immediate family in tow, and then, the other deer — bucks included — would tag along soon after.

Lott and Hart's studies of the Fulani culture clarify how Master Herders use this knowledge for optimal herd management. While they spend most of their day in Nurturer/Companion and Sentinel activities, they consciously choose between dominance and leadership when they must protect or move individuals and groups. Once I understood this concept — and I truly learned this from ethnological research on this particular African tribe — my ability to not just train but socialize my own horses took a quantum leap in effectiveness. And I began to see the parallels in working with people, which excited me to no end.

However, the initial step of recognizing the *difference between* the behavior of a herd Leader and the antics of a herd Dominant marks *the* turning point in understanding how to deal effectively with groups of mobile, empowered humans, whether they be employees, colleagues, constituents, or family members. Anyone who proposes to lead or parent passionate, opinionated people must refrain from taking the power plays of Dominants personally, while teaching them how to adopt the mature, beneficial form of this potentially explosive role. (In this effort, it's helpful to review the four "power principles" in chapter 3, pages 86–97.)

## Step Seven: Move with the Herd

Joe Hutto's chronicles of life with the mule deer are invaluable in understanding the most likely sequence of events our pastoral cousins followed when forming close partnerships with unrestrained, socially intelligent herbivores. Among many surprising insights, the naturalist's experience confirms why humans pretty much *had to* progress from loose, mutually respectful associations at some form of agricultural oasis, to close bonding through touch and caring for the herd's most vulnerable members, and finally, to increasing synchronization with the herd's nomadic lifestyle.

As it turns out, the deer never would have let Hutto anywhere near them if he had tried to approach them on the range first. Several years into this interspecies adventure, he gained the ability to join the herd off-property, but this came about through his close association with the orphaned doe Peep. Hutto admits that Peep was "partially imprinted on me, or at least desperately in need of someone. Without a mother, she knew only that life was not on her side, but she had recently learned that I was the only being who was fully invested in her unlikely and fragile little life."

One day, as twenty deer were heading out toward the north meadow, Hutto "thoughtlessly stayed at Peep's side as she browsed along." Fifteen minutes later, he realized they were a quarter mile from the house. The other deer were curious, if a little nervous about this new development, but Hutto respected the breakthrough as one of many small miracles that allowed him greater access to the mule deer's secret life. For the next few weeks, Hutto continued his evening walks with the herd, but he was able to move with them only if he followed specific individuals who welcomed his presence.

> I found that if I tried to approach the deer after they had left the compound without me, they would become uncomfortable, and some would start to move away. But as long as I was "among" the deer, they seemed to remain at ease and appeared entirely unaffected by my presence.

This, in turn, inspired yet another breakthrough with individuals who had remained suspicious or fearful of Joe and Leslye at the house. As the intrepid naturalist milled around with the herd out in the field, more reticent deer began to relax. At first, they seemed to be ignoring their strange two-legged mascot. But slowly, casually, they made their way closer and closer, eventually browsing around his feet. These deer, Hutto realized, "were more comfortable with me in their world than when they had been with me, in mine." Yet he clearly had to be invited into this world by does and fawns that more nervous deer trusted.

It took even longer for Hutto to successfully join up with the deer in remote locations. To this day, the animals show extreme caution when he approaches, even at a half mile. They begin to walk away from him at a quarter mile unless he initiates an "identifying call." Even after they recognize him,

> deer etiquette requires an indirect, leisurely, meandering approach, with eyes more often averted. And rather than barging into the group, I will slowly work my way into their vicinity and then allow them to gradually work in around me, as I am often joined and greeted by a few of the more familiar individuals. Obviously, my direct proximity to any deer is a significant source of reassurance and a consolation to other deer in the distance. After a few minutes of curious stares by a few of the

more tentative individuals, I am assimilated into the herd, and my presence is no longer a source of concern.

At this point, Hutto realized that he had to raise his Sentinel skills considerably. To safely move among the mule deer, he had to develop a relaxed yet heightened awareness of the environment. He had to simultaneously pay attention to the moods and constantly changing proximity of his fellow herd members as well as to the arrival on the scene of the occasional human, predator, or unfamiliar mule deer buck.

On more than one occasion, a silhouette has suddenly appeared on the far horizon as a distinctly human form, and I have almost been trampled by the explosive flight that has occurred. This flight response is one of only two scenarios in which I have ever felt in danger of bodily harm from these animals. The other is the rare occasion when two dominant bucks — one nearly always a stranger — engage in mortal combat. Often with no preliminary posturing or gesturing, an enormous deer seems to come out of nowhere. The power and violence unleashed is unimaginable when experienced at closer range, and they are oblivious to anything that stands in their way....

Interestingly, the innate fear that is hardwired into almost all predators regarding a human presence is disturbingly absent when I am in the company of deer. This is a privileged perspective when the goshawk or the bald eagle perches thirty meters away, but disconcerting when the mountain lion appears. There is an old saying in this part of the West: "You don't have to be faster than the bear — you just have to be faster than the other guy." Invariably after the deer have scattered, I am left standing face to face with the source of their flight.... When in the field with these deer, I may be seen with a rifle slung over my shoulder — for my protection and theirs — and I have not hesitated to use it on more than one occasion.

Still, after all the small steps that led to the huge inroads Hutto made with the mule deer clan, he veered decisively from the trajectory of what our pastoralist ancestors further achieved. Partly because he's a modern man with a wife and a job, partly because he and Leslye had already pushed the boundaries of what is, in the state of Wyoming, considered legal in their interactions with wild animals, Hutto did not fully merge with the herd and follow them on their summer migrations. Still, the experience changed him forever.

> Now when a bullet passes through the body of one of my family members, or a throat is pierced by the teeth of a 180-pound cat, there is no more displacement or refuge from my attachment — that mindless, objective space where previously my emotions would have safely resided.... I now realize that the objective, safe haven wherein we conveniently assign all unpleasantness in this world — "the natural order of things" — was always a house of cards, merely a childish and inadequate domain lacking a fundamental grasp of a more wondrous and confounding, but stark and undeniably pernicious, reality.

Joining with any group of free, intelligent beings calls for courage, responsiveness, and not just compassion, but an empathy that becomes especially painful when you realize you may not be able to change the destiny of those you grow to love. It takes a strong heart to stay with them nonetheless and do what you can to protect, support, and value each life, no matter how short someone's time on this earth may be, no matter how peaceful or tragic the ending. *This* is what made George Washington such an exceptional figure. Far too many people are more willing to put their lives on the line physically than explore the emotional dimensions of existence. Historically, those with leadership ambitions have found it easier to shut down their hearts, objectify the "other," control the behavior of the masses, and limit *everyone's* options, including the capacity of those "in charge" to reach *their* full potential.

## Step Eight: Move the Herd

As Joe Hutto found, caring for each individual as profoundly as you *must care* to gain the herd's trust requires an emotional heroism that is inconceivable to the civilized psyche. Yet some of our ancestors took that journey, learning not only how to move with the herd, but how to *merge* with the herd. Then, and only then, did they have any hope of *moving* the herd. But they had to pay a price, one that no amount of money can ever buy: They had to leave their egos at the gate while riding a relentless rollercoaster of intense joy, ecstatic discovery, growing power, mind-bending fear, deep pain, and at times, profound helplessness.

To access the knowledge that primeval pastoralists acquired and modern city dwellers neglect, we too must relinquish our most beloved notions of superiority and be transformed by those we wish to influence. In the process, we must learn how to wield power as a socializing force, taking cues from the examples nature provided in freely roaming animals millennia before we learned how to restrain and corral them.

A Master Herder is first and foremost the master of his or her own mind and heart. Courageous enough to simultaneously stand up to and be deeply moved by those he or she leads, such a person is ultimately willing to embrace an improvisatory life that flows from the wisdom, needs, and talents of a fully empowered herd.

# Master Herder Professional Assessment

The following assessment is designed to measure which roles you employ in *professional settings*. Because your job description and the culture of the company or organization you work for is likely to influence your behavior, it's important to take the test with a specific organization in mind. For instance, if you are a bank manager who also serves on the board of a local nonprofit, you should take the test two times to measure how you show up in each setting. (See Julie Bridge's experience of how different jobs lead to different assessments, pages 170–173.)

This assessment is designed for work, educational or community-related situations, and volunteer positions. To measure which roles you employ with your spouse, children, parents, and other family members or friends, see the Personal Relationship Assessment offered on the website www.masterherder.com.

## Assessment Instructions

Complete the following self-assessment by giving your honest answer to how you would most likely respond in each of the scenarios in the chart. Consider the intention of each of the responses and determine the likelihood of you responding in the manner presented, even if you wouldn't use the exact wording. Answering honestly will assist you in finding out more about which Master Herder role or roles you tend to adopt in that particular professional setting.

First, read the "Scenario," then read each possible response in rows A through E. Rate each of the five responses (A–E) based on the likelihood that you would respond in that way. Use numbers 1 to 4, based on these responses:

1: This rating indicates that you are "highly unlikely to ever respond that way."

2: This indicates that, though you wouldn't rule it out, especially as a last resort, you probably would *not* respond that way.

3: This indicates that while you may not agree with the attitude expressed in this response, you will sometimes take the action described if the situation calls for it.

4: This indicates that you are highly likely to respond that way.

As you can see, none of the ratings are categorical. They reflect tendencies. This is because each scenario and your response might differ depending on the specific context and people involved. Consider these variations as you rate each response. In essence, the middle scores indicate that you lean toward or away from that response more often than not.

Here is an example of how someone might rate the first scenario: row A = 4; row B = 1; row C = 1; row D = 4; and row E = 3. Notice that rows A and D have the same rating of 4. This indicates that the person is most likely to engage either one of these responses depending upon the situation or even that the person often combines the two. Notice that rows B and C have the same rating of 1; this indicates that the person is highly unlikely to respond in either of these ways. Row E has a rating of 3, which indicates that the person *might* respond this way. No columns have a rating of 2. Thus, it is expected that each scenario will have two or more responses with the same rating, and that some ratings may not be used. Each scenario response should be rated independently, not scored relative to the others.

## Scenario 1

You've received unfortunate news, and you anticipate a negative reaction/emotion when you communicate it to others.

| | |
|---|---|
| **A = __** | Tell it like it is. Don't beat around the bush. Once the bad news is revealed, you can watch and see how individuals respond and deal with them directly so the group doesn't get out of control. |
| **B = __** | Share bits and pieces slowly and methodically so that there isn't panic and upset that create stress for individuals. Allow bits of information to sink in before adding another piece. |
| **C = __** | Focus on the bigger picture of what is important and why things will turn out for the better if everyone involved also focuses on future opportunities. |
| **D = __** | Be careful to protect leadership from looking badly to avoid a potential crisis. Instead, craft a message that downplays the extent of bad news and keeps some aspects of the news unrevealed. Information is given on a need-to-know basis. |
| **E = __** | Wait on communicating the news to see if perhaps the situation will change. It's no use getting others upset until you absolutely have to – better to wait and see and hope that nothing at all will have to be done. |

## Scenario 2

Two individuals in your area of control are having an interpersonal conflict that has been going on for some time. Others are aware of it, and it is now impacting productivity.

| | |
|---|---|
| **A = __** | Meet with each individual informally and sympathize with each person's perspective. Encourage them to reach out to each other and find a way to resolve the conflict. |
| **B = __** | Bring the two individuals together and give a verbal or written warning to both of them. Reiterate that such behavior will not be tolerated and that they are expendable. |
| **C = __** | Keep an eye on the conflict but don't intervene at this time. Allow the conflict to run its natural course. Most likely it will dissipate soon. It might be more damaging to put a spotlight on it, which could create more conflict and could be even worse for productivity. |
| **D = __** | At a team meeting, call attention to the conflict and use this as an example to the rest of the team of what cannot be tolerated if productivity is to remain high. |
| **E = __** | Meet with each individual separately. Explain that due to the conflict, productivity is suffering, which is impacting the bottom line. Appeal to their dedication to the success of the business to resolve it. |

## Scenario 3

Your organization is going to be doing a major technology upgrade, which will impact systems and processes over the next year. You need to manage the concerns people have regarding the changes and how their jobs will be impacted.

| | |
|---|---|
| **A = ___** | Remind everyone that growth of the business is critical for the business to survive, so there is no excuse for not getting on board with the change and working hard to acquire the skills required to be competent. |
| **B = ___** | Don't call attention to the changes other than to discuss the tactical requirements and expectations. |
| **C = ___** | Announce the changes, also recognizing that this may be a good time to identify those who continue to push back on accepting the organization's need for innovation. Individuals will be watched to see how they manage the changes. If they are resistant or undermine the process, they will be asked to leave. |
| **D = ___** | Help individuals see the bigger picture related to the upgrade. Emphasize how it will increase efficiency across business units despite the steep learning curve. |
| **E = ___** | Find out who is struggling with the upgrade, listen to their concerns, and offer support in the way of additional training and one-on-one coaching so that they feel confident and competent with the changes. |

## Scenario 4

A crisis creates a huge amount of stress across the organization, and it is affecting productivity or the ability to reach business results.

| | |
|---|---|
| **A = ___** | The crisis will offer a good opportunity to sit back and observe who is capable of managing their stress and remaining productive despite the crisis and who uses the crisis to elevate their stress and justify their loss of productivity. |
| **B = ___** | Remind individuals that stress is inevitable and that bad things happen, but that is not a reason to stop being accountable and responsible for their job duties. Emphasize that it is time to "get back to work." |
| **C = ___** | Offer individuals who are really suffering from the stress of the crisis an opportunity to take personal time. Create extra time in your schedule for one-on-one coaching, and actively check in with individuals across the business until the stress subsides. |
| **D = ___** | Notice who handles the crisis reasonably well. Identify those who have trouble managing the stress from the crisis and consider that they may be a liability to the organization going forward and may need to be considered for a layoff or termination. |
| **E = ___** | Take the time to acknowledge the cause of the stress but don't dwell on it. Then offer a vision of innovations or resolutions that will inspire and motivate others to move forward. Trust that HR and/or managers will handle individual needs. |

## Scenario 5

Some aspect of the business is not functioning optimally, such as reporting errors, customer service issues, or loss of revenue. You realize that interpersonal dynamics are the cause.

| | |
|---|---|
| A = __ | Meet with the individuals who are engaged in the interpersonal conflict and give a verbal and written warning that their behavior is not acceptable. Make it clear that you will not hesitate to put them on probation if the matter is not cleared up immediately. |
| B = __ | Meet with the staff and talk at a high level about how everyone needs to work together despite differences in the hope that those who need to will hear the message. |
| C = __ | Wait and see if the dynamics shift over a reasonable period of time. Often it is something petty. Though you will definitely watch what happens, why stir things up further by putting attention on it now? |
| D = __ | Get to the bottom of why this is occurring in a staff meeting. Identify which individuals need to be confronted about their unprofessional behavior. At the same time, give everyone the message that it is time to put an end to these shenanigans and focus on the business. |
| E = __ | In a staff meeting, remind everyone that the reason they work here is to help the organization thrive so that they can be proud of their efforts. Then go on to point out that interpersonal issues and conflict clearly impact the bottom line, so everybody has to make an effort to work well together. |

## Scenario 6

You are experiencing interpersonal conflict with someone who reports to you.

| | |
|---|---|
| A = __ | This insubordination cannot be allowed to continue or others will begin to act out in similar ways. Let the individual know that his or her lack of respect for you must change for the better immediately. |
| B = __ | Why would you want someone on your team who doesn't respect you? Give this person a verbal and written warning. |
| C = __ | Without calling this person out or putting him or her on the spot, tell the entire staff that you want to know if someone has issues with you because – as a team – interpersonal issues will get in the way of the bigger vision for the organization. |
| D = __ | Set up a one-on-one coaching session with the individual and point out his or her strengths and positive contributions. Ask the person to share any concerns he or she may have about you as the manager. |
| E = __ | Let this person know that your door is open if there's something he or she wants to discuss with you – then give it some time. The individual may be going through a personal challenge, and his or her behavior and attitude will eventually change. |

## Scenario 7

A business decision has resulted in reducing the number of employees. This has created a strain on others, who now need to take on more job duties.

| | |
|---|---|
| A = __ | Remind employees that in many companies, once an initial downsizing occurs, future ones are easier to execute. This is a fight to keep the company afloat. Those who excel during this challenge will be rewarded. |
| B = __ | Wait and see if employees become discontent with the change. They may be willing to work harder in order to keep their jobs and keep the business viable. |
| C = __ | Take the time to meet with each area to assess people's concerns over extended job duties. Offer support through training and coaching. Let people know that your door is always open to address more personal concerns. Create some ongoing incentives for doing a good job. |
| D = __ | Remind remaining staff that the decision, while difficult, was necessary for the business to move forward. Offer examples of other companies that went through a similar reorganization and subsequently excelled. |
| E = __ | Remind staff that management has kept them on, following a downsizing, because they were seen as the capable and competent ones. Tell them you have every confidence that they can manage the change in workload. |

## Scenario 8

Underperforming individuals will most likely become very upset when you meet with them to give them feedback.

| | |
|---|---|
| A = __ | Tell them exactly what they need to do to receive a higher evaluation next time. Point out that they must keep it together and not appear weak or unable to handle such feedback if they are interested in future promotions or opportunities. |
| B = __ | Wait until their quarterly performance review to provide the feedback formally. Email their evaluation to them, so you don't have to deal with them being upset, and wait and see what they do. |
| C = __ | Meet with them and point out that becoming upset when receiving feedback is a ploy to avoid being criticized, and it doesn't work with you. They must learn to take feedback from management and make changes to perform up to expectations. |
| D = __ | Meet with them and counsel them on their sensitivity to hearing performance feedback. Let them know you understand how difficult it can be and that you will support them in doing better in the future. |
| E = __ | Begin by sharing with them a time when you received a poor evaluation and how it became an opportunity to improve so that they can see there is a positive opportunity for them going forward. |

## Scenario 9
**You have interpersonal issues with people you report to.**

| | |
|---|---|
| **A = __** | Find a time to talk informally to let them know how much you respect them and appreciate their guidance. Ask if there is anything they'd like you to do differently. |
| **B = __** | Meet with them and share with them your vision of how you'd like to see the two of you working together and express your hope that things will begin to change. |
| **C = __** | Take control of the situation by communicating your concerns, being completely honest about how you see the situation and how you would like it resolved. |
| **D = __** | Let them know that this ongoing issue is getting in the way of you doing your job. Let them know that if this conflict continues, your work may be compromised and that you have other places in mind where you know you will be valued. |
| **E = __** | See if they bring it up, otherwise you might be making a big deal out of nothing. Maybe your perception is wrong and there is no issue. |

## Scenario 10
**Individuals who report to you are constantly complaining about everything and everyone.**

| | |
|---|---|
| **A = __** | Give them an alternative: Either they discontinue their complaining or they will be removed from their current positions and placed on probation, with termination as an option. |
| **B = __** | Meet with them and remind them that the organization cannot be successful if the culture becomes one of complaining. Ask them if they see how damaging it can be to the business. |
| **C = __** | Attempt to cheer them up and alleviate their reasons for complaining – pointing out the good aspects of things and people. Help them find ways to feel motivated and excited about their work. |
| **D = __** | Avoid interactions with them in the hopes that, by being marginalized, they'll get the hint and will stop this behavior. |
| **E = __** | Make playfully sarcastic comments about their complaining to others in their presence and confront them in front of their peers – making them a public example to others of what will not be tolerated. |

## Scenario 11

**When you are angry at work about something or someone, you do the following.**

| | |
|---|---|
| **A = ___** | Seek to feel good again by acting as if anger is no big deal and showing others that you don't appear angry even though you are. If they ask if you are angry, you say, "No." |
| **B = ___** | Use the anger to get what you want from others. Express it without reservation, which will motivate others to respond to you immediately. |
| **C = ___** | Immerse yourself in a project or report, or in big-picture thinking, in order to ignore and avoid this strong feeling, in the hopes that what is causing the anger will resolve itself. |
| **D = ___** | Move to express the feeling of anger by confronting the situation and taking control of it – even if you have to be harsh in some instances. |
| **E = ___** | Use the anger to motivate you to look at the situation and make some changes in policy, process, or personnel. The anger cues you to take some sort of action that will change the current situation. |

## Scenario 12

**When you are frustrated at work about something or someone, you do the following.**

| | |
|---|---|
| **A = ___** | Focus on solution-seeking for the frustration. Look at the bigger picture of why the frustration is occurring, and try to create a new view of the situation. Relief comes by creating something new or different to focus on. |
| **B = ___** | Keep the frustration to yourself in order to avoid upsetting anybody. However, you keep the reason for the frustration alive, so you don't just let it go as insignificant. |
| **C = ___** | Move to taking control of the frustration by directly addressing a person or a situation. There is little concern about how others will respond or feel because something must be done. |
| **D = ___** | Figure out who or what is causing the frustration and confront it. You are willing to eliminate the reason without concern for the fallout from such a decision. |
| **E = ___** | Pull back and take a position of watching and waiting to see if the situation or person changes with time, which will then relieve your frustration. |

## Scenario 13

**When you are feeling vulnerable at work about something or someone, you do the following.**

| | |
|---|---|
| **A = ___** | Retreat from the situation or avoid the person and wait and see if something changes, so that the feeling will dissipate. |
| **B = ___** | Look at what is going on in the organization that is causing this emotional response and ask others if they share similar feelings. |
| **C = ___** | Immediately seek to gain back a sense of being in control while keeping others from knowing about your feeling of vulnerability. |
| **D = ___** | Feeling vulnerable is a weakness and not ever appropriate to show or admit because it gives the competition an edge. |
| **E = ___** | Seek out others who will offer you support, reminding you of the strengths and abilities you have, as well as offer solutions to the situation. |

## Scenario 14

**When you need help or support at work for either a work-related issue or interpersonal issue, you do the following.**

| | |
|---|---|
| **A = ___** | Don't expect others to take care of your needs, even though it would be nice. You are the one who should be caring for others – not drawing attention to yourself. |
| **B = ___** | Make sure everyone knows what you need, and see to it that they meet those needs for you so that you can maintain a sense of control. |
| **C = ___** | Don't bother others with your needs. Stay focused on creating and envisioning the future and deal with your needs on your own. |
| **D = ___** | Watch and see if anybody recognizes that you need help or support. If they offer it, accept it, but don't ask for it. |
| **E = ___** | Never let them see you sweat. Asking for support or having others meet your needs is a sign of weakness. |

## Master Herder Professional Assessment Scoring Sheet

Copy the scoring sheet on the next page so you can use it multiple times. For each scenario, enter the numeric value you assigned to the letter on the Master Herder Professional Assessment. Note that the scoring sheet rearranges the order of the assessment's lettered responses for each scenario. For instance, to continue the example used above, if someone in the first scenario rated the row C response with a 1, then the first row of the scoring sheet would read C = 1, and so on. For each scenario, fill in all the numeric ratings, ensuring they match the lettered rows on the assessment.

Once all the numeric values are entered, add up each of the five columns, putting the totals at the bottom. For advice on how to interpret the assessment, read the section following the scoring sheet.

| Scenario | LEADER | NURTURER/ COMPANION | DOMINANT | SENTINAL | PREDATOR |
|---|---|---|---|---|---|
| 1 | C = | B = | A = | E = | D = |
| 2 | E = | A = | D = | C = | B = |
| 3 | D = | E = | A = | B = | C = |
| 4 | E = | C = | B = | A = | D = |
| 5 | E = | B = | D = | C = | A = |
| 6 | C = | D = | A = | E = | B = |
| 7 | D = | C = | E = | B = | A = |
| 8 | E = | D = | A = | B = | C = |
| 9 | B = | A = | C = | E = | D = |
| 10 | B = | C = | E = | D = | A = |
| 11 | E = | A = | D = | C = | B = |
| 12 | A = | B = | C = | E = | D = |
| 13 | B = | E = | C = | A = | D = |
| 14. | C = | A = | E = | D = | B = |
| Total | | | | | |

## Interpreting the Results

The Master Herder Professional Assessment is designed to highlight the roles that you overemphasize or avoid, as well as acknowledge the roles you are currently balancing well. Scores that fall within three points of each other indicate your tendency to balance those roles. Scores that are unusually high or unusually low in relation to the others are important to consider more carefully.

In relation to your highest score, it's helpful to notice when you're employing the strengths and benefits of this role in its mature form, and when you're lapsing into the challenges (and therefore dysfunctional behaviors) of the role. The latter often occurs because you are either naturally talented or well trained in this role (and therefore tend to use it as your default system), or because your position encourages you to overemphasize it. Remember that, depending on the organizational culture and the details of your job description, outside forces may cause you to overemphasize certain roles. For instance, if you work in acquisitions and mergers, you're likely to score high in the Predator role because your position involves deciding whom to lay off (cull). If you work in a field related to social work and mental health, you're likely to exhibit a high Nurturer/Companion score. If you created the corporation or nonprofit you now work for, you're more likely to overemphasize the Leader role. Law enforcement and military personnel are more inclined to stress the Dominant and Sentinel roles.

In the case of your lowest score, reflect on how the organization may suffer from your tendency to avoid that particular role. For instance, people who abdicate the Dominant role have trouble getting resistant staff members back on task, moderating conflict, and curtailing dysfunctional group and interpersonal dynamics. Those who overemphasize the Nurturer/Companion role in particular are often surprised to find that they score higher in the Predator role than in the Dominant role. This occurs when naturally caring people avoid conflict and habitually employ a soft and understanding approach, refusing to engage the strong, directive power of the Dominant when needed. As a result, Nurturer/Companions in supervisory positions may eventually end up firing employees who "just don't get it" rather than handling the discomfort of curtailing unproductive behavior as it arises, holding people accountable, and firmly directing them to adopt more functional interpersonal skills and work habits.

In most jobs, the Predator role should exhibit a lower score than all the others. Employing it thoughtfully and sparingly most often involves using it as a methodical, predictable last resort with staff members who have not responded to a crescendo of interactions based on the other roles. For instance, getting an aggressive or resistant employee back on track would first involve employing supportive, trust-building Nurturer/Companion skills, followed by a frank, no-nonsense Sentinel conversation outlining how the employee's behavior is affecting the team and the organization as a whole. If little progress were made, you would then crescendo into the Leader role, perhaps by engaging a more directive yet still inspirational approach illuminating how the employee's talents would benefit the company — if the dysfunctional behavior were promptly corrected. But some people truly need the solid backbone and increasingly stern "pushing" energy of the Dominant as an impetus to change their ways. The Dominant would also inform a still-errant staff member that the next step involves termination. If the employee ignored this warning after all the previous efforts to help him or her to correct the objectionable behavior, the Predator would emerge to carry out the predicted firing firmly, unemotionally, and without apology.

Even though it is most often the lowest number on the Master Herder scale, a reasonable Predator score falls in the 20s. People who score less than 18 for this role are more likely to abdicate the Predator role, which can be problematic. Refusing to cull staff members who've been given a crescendo of chances to correct their behavior will breed resentment and apathy in high-functioning staff. And in tough economic climates, waiting too long to cut programs and lay off a smaller number of employees might cause the entire company to fold, resulting in all staff members losing their jobs.

There are many meaningful variations in the Master Herder Professional Assessment scores. For this reason, I have specifically trained some of my instructors in this model to offer phone consultations on what the assessment shows. Please see www.masterherder.com for a list of approved instructors who can not only help you interpret the results, but also offer specific training to help you improve in the areas you may overemphasize or avoid.

# Acknowledgments

First of all, I'd like to thank every challenging person, horse, or dog I've ever met for inspiring me to ask the essential questions that led to writing this book. I'm doubly grateful to the human colleagues, herd members, and pack members who created a supportive learning environment during my sometimes-tempestuous search for answers. Often the line between the "challengers" and the "supporters" blurred. In collaborating with my most adventurous two- and four-legged associates, I slowly recognized, codified, and experimented with moving fluidly among all five of the Master Herder roles. In the process, it became clear that none of us should be limited or defined by our favorite behavior patterns. Balancing the various forms of power ultimately involves embracing a much wider vision of who we truly are as we discover, time and time again, that even our greatest talents can result in dysfunction when we overidentify with certain roles.

Recognizing the unproductive aspects of each role helps people make sense of otherwise confusing group dynamics. But until colleagues, bosses, family, and community members achieve a reasonable balance of their own, it can be quite a juggling act — even for those well versed in the Master Herder model — to negotiate the antics of overtly aggressive Dominants, stealthy Predators, passive-aggressive

Nurturer/Companions, secretive or hypervigilant Sentinels, and disconnected or self-possessed Leaders.

Still, completing this manuscript somehow felt even more challenging to me for one simple, perpetually irritating reason. Whenever I sat down to write, I was gripped by the evolution of a frustrating cliché: if "a picture is worth a thousand words," then a single experience is worth at least a thousand pictures. As a result, presenting this model in person is *much* easier than writing about it. During indoor seminars on the Five Roles of a Master Herder, lively discussions take place, inspired by the participants' personal anecdotes as well as by photos and videos of animals who exemplify certain roles. I also point out various dynamics through images of traditional herding cultures facing situations that clearly call for the expert use of each and every role. In equine-facilitated workshops that exercise these skills, participants *experience* the benefits of roles they might otherwise avoid, while also practicing how to more appropriately employ roles they overemphasize.

Translating all this visual, verbal, and nonverbal information to the written page was a vigorous and perplexing journey, one that would not have been possible without the input, encouragement, and hard work of the many wonderful people who supported me as I struggled with this task. My husband, Steve Roach, was a constant source of strength, wisdom, and energy through the ups and downs of completing this project. I'm deeply grateful to barn manager Elysa Ginsburg and the dedicated staff members who made sure that our horses were taken care of 24/7: Nyla Schaffner, Lucinda Vette, Tyler and Haley Schaffner, Rafael Carruthers, Caitlin Hudecek, Frank Schaffner, Frank Schaffner, Jr., Vanessa Schafer, Erin Menut, and Yongkai Ow. In various capacities, these people managed the farm, exercised and nurtured the horses, and helped facilitate workshops during the time I researched and wrote about the five roles. Office manager Sue Smades took over many of the business details I normally handle to free up concentrated writing time. Theresa Alvarez provided crucial workshop support.

The Master Herder model also benefited from the input and questions of Eponaquest instructors who were members of three different facilitator-training classes that were learning to present this model during the time I was writing this book. Members of Apprenticeship Class 23 helped me to create the PowerPoint presentation that became the outline for this book: Julie Bridge, Laura Day, Dunia Dubon de Morales, Cyndie Hays, Cecile Lavault, Lauren Loos, Alane Millions, Willow Moore, and Diana Will.

Class 28 helped to perfect the accompanying equine-facilitated activities: Lori Cohen, Leslie Iles, Sarah Janosik, Erin Menut, Charlotte Richardson, and Angela Wilken. Special thanks go to Class 28 member Terri Roberson for coming up with the phrase *dominance without malice* during her powerful interactions with my feisty little dominant horse Spirit.

And finally, members of Class 31 were pioneers in helping Juli Lynch and me further hone the Master Herder Professional Assessment: Laurie Baker, Hélène Bernier, Susan Crimmins, Andrea Klein, Meg Knowles, Sasha Levy, Janet Murray, Yongkai Ow, Nancy Proulx, Lucinda Vette, and Roxy Wright.

I was very impressed with the French Eponaquest instructors. They worked together as a high-level team of empowered, mutually supportive colleagues in organizing my 2015 tour of France to support *The Power of the Herd* translation into their language as well as to introduce the Master Herder model to their fellow countrymen and -women. Cecile Gilbert-Kawano did an excellent job of acting as translator for that monthlong series of events.

Special thanks to Lorraine Tilbury for connecting me with Didier Tranchier, head of the Executive MBA program "Leading Innovation in a Digital World" at the l'Institut Mines-Telecom in Paris, where I presented this model to an enthusiastic, multilingual audience of entrepreneurs and business students in 2014.

I'm grateful to my colleague Carol Roush for taking the Eponaquest work to Europe to begin with, and to Sabine Heimen, Beatrice Hunkeler, Christiane Lottgen, and Elke Wedig for organizing, translating, and helping to facilitate several related events in Germany.

Three other Eponaquest colleagues introduced me to key concepts and books that enhanced my research: Mary-Louise Gould was invaluable in helping define the benefits and challenges of the Sentinel role; Thea Fast brought Kropotkin's concept of "mutual aid as a factor of evolution" to my attention; and Martina Danzer sent me a link to the book *The Art and Science of Shepherding: Tapping the Wisdom of French Herders*.

A very special thank-you to my Eponaquest instructor colleague Sharon Alley for introducing me to the work of sociometrist Greg Reid.

I would also like to thank Bill and Margaret Couch, Juli Lynch, Dr. Rebecca Bailey, Shelley Rosenberg, Elizabeth and William Shatner, Meg Daley Olmert, Kathleen McGarry, Rob Bensman, Katherine Marine, and Trisha Schaffner for their wisdom, enthusiasm, and support at various points along the way.

As always, my editor, Jason Gardner, was an invaluable source of clarity in helping me to better hone the sometimes-complex insights presented in this book. Copyeditor Jeff Campbell and proofreader Tanya Fox also provided crucial input on content and accuracy. Thanks to my agent, Felicia Eth, who was very supportive of this venture.

It's impossible to list all the students, apprentices, instructors, and friends who helped me gain deeper understanding of dynamics leading to the creation of the Master Herder model. I have been touched and inspired by their willingness to explore these sometimes-uncomfortable, ultimately empowering insights and tools. I'm also deeply indebted to my herd and to the horses worldwide whom I encountered during my journeys.

And to you, the reader, who makes all the work worthwhile. May the wisdom, spirit, and power of the horse accompany you through all of life's adventures.

# Endnotes

## Preface

Page 2, *One ambitious study, undertaken by UC Berkeley:* Gregory J. Feist and Frank Barron, "Emotional Intelligence and Academic Intelligence in Career and Life Success," paper presented at the Annual Convention of the American Psychological Society, San Francisco, June 1996, quoted in Bob Wall, *Working Relationships: Using Emotional Intelligence to Enhance Your Effectiveness with Others* (Mountain View, CA: Davies-Black Publishing, 1999, 2008), 27.

Page 2, *"IQ and training get you in the arena":* Bob Wall quoted during his 2008 workshop in Sonoita, AZ, hosted by Linda Kohanov.

## Introduction

Page 17, *"things are not only changing":* Jason Ankeny, "20/20 Visions," *Entrepreneur* (January 2015): 38.

Page 17, *"very entrepreneurial and tend to have a lot":* Ibid., 35.

Page 17, *"mutual benefit partnering":* Ibid., 34.

Page 18, *"lateral power organized nodally":* Jeremy Rifkin, *The Third Industrial Revolution: How Lateral Power Is Transforming Energy, the Economy, and the World* (New York: Palgrave Macmillan, 2011), 139.

Page 22, Inc. *magazine's editor-at-large Leigh Buchanan divides:* Leigh Buchanan, "The De-Machoing of Great Leadership," *Inc.com* (June 2013), http://www.inc.com/magazine/201306/leigh-buchanan/leadership-era -which-was-most-successful.html.

Page 22, *"as he attacks competitors":* Ibid.

Page 22, *"rely on store-level employees"*: Ibid.

Page 22, *"dons an apron and serves snacks"*: Ibid.

Page 22, *"Increasingly,"* Buchanan asserts, *"the chief executive role"*: Leigh Buchanan, "Between Venus and Mars: 7 Traits of True Leaders," *Inc.com* (June 2013), http://www.inc.com/magazine/201306/leigh-buchanan/traits-of -true-leaders.html.

Page 23, *"a man for our times"*: Ibid.

Page 23, *"Let your heart feel for the affliction"*: William J. Bennett, ed., *Our Sacred Honor: Words of Advice from the Founders in Stories, Letters, Poems, and Speeches* (New York: Simon and Schuster, 1997), 162.

Page 24, *"I see their situation, know their danger"*: George Washington, *The Writings of George Washington*, ed. Worthington Chauncey Ford (New York: G. P. Putnam's Sons, 1889), 1:249–50.

## Chapter One. Evolution of Power

Page 32, *"I failed to find — although I was eagerly looking for it"*: Peter Alekseevich Kropotkin, *Mutual Aid: A Factor of Evolution*, 1st ed. (London: William Heinemann, 1902), vii.

Page 32, *"could agree with none of the works"*: Ibid., ix, x.

Page 32, *"The first thing which strikes us"*: Ibid, 38, 57.

Page 34, *"There is no fundamental difference between man and"*: Charles Darwin, *The Works of Charles Darwin*, eds. Paul H. Barrett and R. B. Freeman, vol. 21, *The Descent of Man, and Selection in Relation to Sex, Part One* (New York: New York University Press, 1989), 70, 73.

Page 35, *"non-human animals have the neuroanatomical, neurochemical"*: "The Cambridge Declaration on Consciousness," eds. Jaak Panksepp, Diana Reiss, David Edelman, Bruno Van Swinderen, Philip Low, and Christof Koch, presented at the Francis Crick Memorial Conference on Consciousness in Human and Non-Human Animals, Churchill College, University of Cambridge, England, July 7, 2012, http://fcmconference.org/img/CambridgeDeclaration OnConsciousness.pdf.

Page 39, *"In the Russian Steppes, [wolves] never attack the horses:* Kropotkin, *Mutual Aid*, 41.

Page 39, *Recently, a horse owner named Talea Morgan-Metivier:* "Cougar in Corral with New Foal," Talea Morgan-Metivier, posted on YouTube, April 29, 2015, https://www.youtube.com/watch?v=QsXgpSt2QMg.

Page 42, *"when given oxytocin, groups of rats"*: Kerstin Uvnäs-Moberg, *The Oxytocin Factor: Tapping the Hormone of Calm, Love, and Healing*, trans. Roberta W. Francis (Cambridge, MA: Da Capo Press, 2003), 66.

Page 43, *"Surprisingly, to a lesser degree, animals that live"*: Ibid., 114.

Page 43, *"The triumph of trust over paranoia"*: Meg Daley Olmert, *Made for Each*

*Other: The Biology of the Human-Animal Bond* (Cambridge, MA: Da Capo Press, 2009), xvi.

Page 43, *"when eighteen men and women interacted with their dogs"*: Ibid., 74.

Page 44, *"Repeated injections of oxytocin in high doses"*: Ibid., 209.

Page 44, *"In our abrupt shift from farm to factory"*: Ibid., 180.

Page 45, *"instills courage by making the individual feel aggressive"*: Uvnäs-Moberg, *The Oxytocin Factor*, 66–67.

Page 47, *"This first art consists of true aesthetic masterpieces"*: David S. Whitley, *Cave Paintings and the Human Spirit: The Origin of Creativity and Belief* (Amherst, NY: Prometheus Books, 2009), 255.

Page 48, "knew *these animals — not just as a species"*: Olmert, *Made for Each Other*, 35.

Page 50, *"Lott was interested in discovering"*: Ibid., 79.

## Chapter Two. Mutual Transformation

Page 55, *"a two-species social system"*: Dale F. Lott and Benjamin L. Hart, "Applied Ethology in a Nomadic Cattle Culture," *Applied Animal Ethology* 5, no. 4 (October 1979): 312.

Page 55, *"the animal of most of the alternatives"*: Ibid., 309.

Page 55, *"is to actively select the desired behavior"*: Ibid.

Page 55, *"may be thought of as taking a social role"*: Ibid., 312.

Page 56, *"Certainly no pushover, he or she knows how to set boundaries"*: Linda Kohanov, *The Power of the Herd: A Nonpredatory Approach to Social Intelligence, Leadership, and Innovation* (Novato, CA: New World Library, 2013), 131–32.

Page 57, *"moving among the cattle at the camps"*: Lott and Hart, "Applied Ethology in a Nomadic Cattle Culture," 316.

Page 58, *"observed several occasions when non-Fulani cattle handlers"*: Dale F. Lott and Benjamin L. Hart, "Aggressive Domination of Cattle by Fulani Herdsmen and Its Relation to Aggression in Fulani Culture and Personality," *Ethos* 5, no. 2 (Summer 1977): 180.

Page 59, *"it is not clear how herdsmen become able"*: Lott and Hart, "Applied Ethology in a Nomadic Cattle Culture," 315.

Page 60, *"Once [the herder] has the cattle's attention"*: Ibid.

Page 60, *"The adaptive value of following a leader"*: Ibid., 314.

Page 60, *"scientific explorations of successful herding practices"*: Michel Meuret and Fred Provenza, eds., *The Art & Science of Shepherding: Tapping the Wisdom of French Herders*, trans. Bruce Inksetter and Melanie Guedenet (Austin, TX: Acres U.S.A., 2014), quote from back flap.

Page 60, *"is based largely on observation"*: Ibid., 362.

Page 61, *"You have to be constantly...on the alert"*: Ibid.

Page 62, *"must be able to anticipate the flock's behavior"*: Ibid.

Page 62, *"a matter of perpetual adjustment between flock"*: Ibid., 363.

Page 62, *"The intimate association between human and sheep"*: Ibid., 365.


### Chapter Four. Discover and Inspire: Leadership through Relationship

Page 107, *"His diary entries reflect his frustration"*: Alan and Donna Jean Fusonie, *George Washington: Pioneer Farmer* (Mount Vernon, VA: Mount Vernon Ladies Association, 1998), 19.

Page 108, *"Two customary methods of separating — or threshing — the wheat"*: Ibid.

Page 108, *"Because of Washington's extended absences"*: Ibid., 20.

Page 109, *"The horses were made to continually run"*: Alex Knapp, "The Five Best Inventions of the Founding Fathers," *Forbes* (July 2011), http://www.forbes .com/sites/alexknapp/2011/07/03/the-five-best-inventions-of-the-founding -fathers/#2edbbf5d1b7d.


### Chapter Five. Support and Connect: The Power of Companionship

Page 122, *"apparently began their penetration of the study area"*: Lott and Hart, "Aggressive Domination of Cattle," 177–78.

Page 123, *"The Fulani's formula of intimacy and aggression"*: Olmert, *Made for Each Other*, 175.


### Chapter Seven. Cull and Recalibrate: The Predator's Sacred Task

Page 152, *"Who killed Youngstown's steel industry"*: "In Youngstown We Made Steel (1977 to present)," anonymous, undated, http://allthingsyoungstown.net /articles/in_youngstown_we_made_steel/article.htm.


### Chapter Eight. Growing Pains

Page 161, *"weaknesses, skill deficiencies, interpersonal shortcomings"*: Patrick Lencioni, *The Five Dysfunctions of a Team: A Leadership Fable* (San Francisco: Jossey-Bass, 2002), 196.

Page 162, *"In the context of building a team"*: Ibid, 195–96.


### Chapter Nine. Working with a Herd: Applications in Real Life

Page 175, *"Just as there was an age of exploration"*: Olmert, *Made for Each Other*, 162.

Page 176, *"focuses not so much on the Fulani's amazing abilities"*: Ibid., 175.

Page 176, *"hard to remember who I once was"*: Joe Hutto, *Touching the Wild: Living with the Mule Deer of Deadman Gulch* (New York: Skyhorse Publishing, 2014), 294.

Page 179, *"We commonly sit on the front porch in the evening"*: Ibid., 12.
Page 179, *"Like chipmunks, many of the bunnies have names"*: Ibid., 10–11.
Page 181, *"As we gazed from the darker interior of the house"*: Ibid., 25–26.
Page 181, *"Rayme had this peculiar habit of staring at us"*: Ibid., 27.
Page 184, *"Soon Rayme became a familiar resident"*: Ibid., 27.
Page 184, *"a profoundly beautiful and elegant deer"*: Ibid., 29.
Page 184, *"Rutting mule deer bucks"*: Ibid., 30.
Page 184, *"immediately identified us as safe neighbors"*: Ibid., 30–31.
Page 186, *"For reasons that will always remain a mystery"*: Ibid., 28.
Page 186, *"Clearly, the new fawns judged from their mothers' demeanor"*: Ibid, 35.
Page 186, *"I still regret not getting to know her better"*: Ibid., 36.
Page 189, *"Leslye exclaimed through the glass"*: Ibid., 37–38.
Page 190, *"Typology,"* a word she uses to describe: Vicki Hearne, *Adam's Task: Calling Animals by Name* (1986; repr., New York: Skyhorse Publishing, 2007), 167.
Page 191, *"training horses creates a logic that demands not only"*: Ibid., 169.
Page 191, *"has found out some things about illiterate peoples"*: Ibid., 170.
Page 191, *"One of his stories was about an eager linguist"*: Ibid.
Page 191, *"not arguing against advances in culture"*: Ibid.
Page 193, *"an egalitarian outlook, without favoritism"*: Natasha Fijn, *Living with Herds: Human-Animal Coexistence in Mongolia* (New York: Cambridge University Press, 2011), 133.
Page 193, *"Mongolians do not eat animals that are under"*: Ibid., 227.
Page 195, *"breached the divide of physical touch"*: Hutto, *Touching the Wild*, 39.
Page 195, *"Like the other deer, if a stranger neared"*: Ibid., 46.
Page 195, *"Her ability to convey meaning to me"*: Ibid.
Page 195, *"I realized that she was not just starved"*: Ibid., 57.
Page 196, *"was naïve and had not yet learned that knowing"*: Ibid., 47.
Page 196, *"Even though Cappy is only one of two hundred"*: Ibid.
Page 197, *"That would invite human imprinting"*: Ibid., 51.
Page 199, *"We saw him pass by a third year"*: Ibid., 32.
Page 200, *"In the midst of constant minor mule deer bickering"*: Ibid., 41–42.
Page 201, *"partially imprinted on me"*: Ibid., 75.
Page 201, *"thoughtlessly stayed at Peep's side"*: Ibid.
Page 202, *"I found that if I tried to approach the deer"*: Ibid., 76.
Page 202, *"were more comfortable with me in their world"*: Ibid.
Page 202, *"deer etiquette requires an indirect"*: Ibid., 81.
Page 203, *"On more than one occasion, a silhouette"*: Ibid., 79.
Page 204, *"Now when a bullet passes through the body"*: Ibid., 294.

# Index

# About the Author

L inda Kohanov is an internationally recognized author, speaker, riding instructor, and horse trainer. In 1997, she founded Epona Equestrian Services, an Arizona-based collective of horse professionals, educators, coaches, and counselors exploring the potential of the horse-human bond. Due to increasing international interest, the business expanded, becoming Eponaquest Worldwide as she and her colleagues trained instructors who now practice on five continents.

Linda is the author of the bestseller *The Tao of Equus*, *Riding between the Worlds*, *The Way of the Horse* (with artist Kim McElroy), and *The Power of the Herd*. Linda's books have been translated into French, German, Dutch, and Czech, and are used as texts at universities throughout the United States.

Linda lectures and conducts workshops at conferences and retreat centers throughout the world, and since 2002, she and her colleagues have trained thousands of people. Seminars at her home base in Amado, Arizona, attract business leaders, entrepreneurs, educators, scientists, mental health professionals, artists, and coaches from around the world. Linda has developed innovative, highly effective approaches to leadership training and team building that have been embraced by executive coaches, sales managers, and major players in the aerospace industry. Starting in 2003, Linda and her colleagues began training instructors capable of leading their own seminars in the Eponaquest approach to equine-facilitated learning. By 2016, close to three hundred Eponaquest instructors from the United States, Canada, Europe, England, Ireland, Australia, South Africa, and Asia had graduated from an apprenticeship program covering the most beneficial practices for enhancing the physical, mental, emotional, and spiritual well-being of their clients.

Linda's main website is www.eponaquest.com. Visit www.master herder.com for more information on the Five Roles of a Master Herder. It features the Master Herder Personal Assessment to help you discover which roles you emphasize and avoid in personal relationships. It also lists the equine-facilitated workshops, indoor seminars, and private consultations that Linda offers featuring this model, as well as instructors worldwide who have completed advanced training with the author in how to teach this model to individuals and groups. A web symposium with in-depth conversations on the material and practical skills presented in her related book *The Power of the Herd* is available at www.poweroftheherd.com.